Fact File
2017

The key facts behind today's issues

All the fac.... DEC 202... ...derstand our world.
In print in this book & online as part of
Complete Issues

Complete Issues
articles · statistics · contacts

FOR REFERENCE ONLY

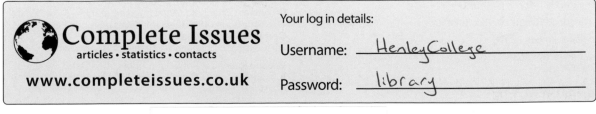

Fact File 2017

The key facts behind today's issues

Fact File 2017 is part of **Complete Issues**, a unique combination of resources online and in print.

Using **www.completeissues.co.uk** you can view individual pages from this book on screen, download, print, use on whiteboards and adapt to suit your needs. It makes Fact File even more flexible and useful.

In addition to the online service, you have this attractive printed version always available. Its clear presentation encourages users to feel confident about using and understanding statistics and to browse and enjoy the data.

Because you have both the book and online access you can use Fact File in different ways with different groups and in different locations. It can be used simultaneously in the library, in the classroom and at home.

You can search for statistics secure in the knowledge that you will find meaningful data from reliable sources.

Your purchase of the book gives you access to Fact File PDFs via Complete Issues on one computer at a time. You can find your access codes on your covering letter or by contacting us. It is useful to record them on page 1 of this volume.

You can upgrade your online Fact File access with the **Online Expansion Pack**. This includes an unlimited site licence to make the service and the material available to all students and staff at all times, even from home. It also unlocks the ability to search this and all your other volumes of Fact File and Essential Articles, and view their contents online as dynamic web pages. You can find details here: www.carelpress.co.uk/factfile

NEW: Interactive graphs

With Fact File 2017 we are introducing interactive graphs to the online service. To access these you will need an **Online Expansion Pack** or to subscribe to **Complete Issues.**

Upgrading to a full **Complete Issues** subscription expands your resources further with combined access to articles, statistics and contacts. In addition, you gain access to our Focus Guides on specific topics - special selections giving you a quick and easy research focus on vital issues.

Complete Issues

Complete Issues gives you the statistics, articles and contacts to understand the world we live in. The unique format means that this information is available on the shelf and on the screen.

For 2017, we have added interactive graphs to Complete Issues, making these vital statistics even more engaging.

How does Complete Issues work?

All the pages are available to view online and download as PDFs and there are references and links to other parts of Complete Issues - the archive of articles, the statistics and the website and contact details of relevant organisations.

The statistics in Fact File, the articles in the Essential Articles series and online contacts work beautifully together on the Complete Issues website to produce a choice of relevant data, opinion and links.

When you search for a topic you instantly generate a list of relevant articles, figures and organisations with a thumbnail of the page and a short description.

The **advantages of Complete Issues** over just googling are:

* varied & reliable sources
* moderated - so appropriate for student use
* properly referenced
* beautifully presented
* ideal for classroom use
* cleared for copyright
* links that are checked for safety and relevance

The **Focus Guides** offer a selection from Complete Issues as a starting point for quick and easy access to information on important topics.

New material is added throughout the year and we will alert you to this and when issues become particularly topical.

If you do not yet have the other resources in Complete Issues - the articles and the contacts - you can sample the service and upgrade here: **www.completeissues.co.uk** or contact us using the details below.

Published by Carel Press Ltd
4 Hewson St, Carlisle CA2 5AU
Tel +44 (0)1228 538928, Fax 591816
office@carelpress.co.uk
www.carelpress.co.uk
© Carel Press

Research, design and editorial team:
Pip Brown, Rachel Carr, Debbie Fuller, Jack Gregory, Christine A Shepherd, Anne Louise Kershaw, Chas White,
Subscriptions: Ann Batey (Manager), Brenda Hughes
Complete Issues Team:
Jack Gregory, Christine A Shepherd, Robbie White

British Library Cataloguing in Publication Data
A catalogue record for this book is available from the British Library

ISBN 978-1-905600-51-9

Printed by Interpress, Budapest

FACT FILE 2017 CONTENTS

"The people we regard as the laziest, rudest, most promiscuous, drunken drug-takers are white men in their twenties."

page 38

"I always felt pressured to do the girls' thing."
page 104

Photo: ©PakistanCBL/ICBL

"More than 6 billion people live in countries where corruption is a serious problem."
page 176

Alcohol, drugs & smoking

Harmful habits

How safe do people think substances are - compared to how safe they actually are?

A YouGov survey of 2,096 GB adults gives an interesting snapshot of what people perceive are the safest and most dangerous drugs.

In your opinion, how SAFE or DANGEROUS is it for a person to use the following substances?

(figures may not add up to 100% due to rounding)

Perception of harm

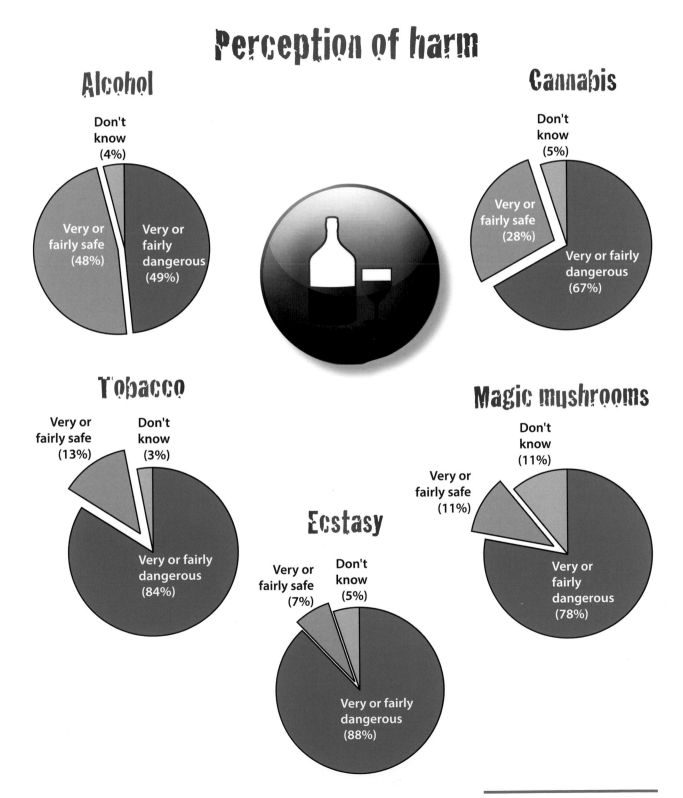

Alcohol

- Don't know (4%)
- Very or fairly safe (48%)
- Very or fairly dangerous (49%)

Cannabis

- Don't know (5%)
- Very or fairly safe (28%)
- Very or fairly dangerous (67%)

Tobacco

- Very or fairly safe (13%)
- Don't know (3%)
- Very or fairly dangerous (84%)

Ecstasy

- Very or fairly safe (7%)
- Don't know (5%)
- Very or fairly dangerous (88%)

Magic mushrooms

- Don't know (11%)
- Very or fairly safe (11%)
- Very or fairly dangerous (78%)

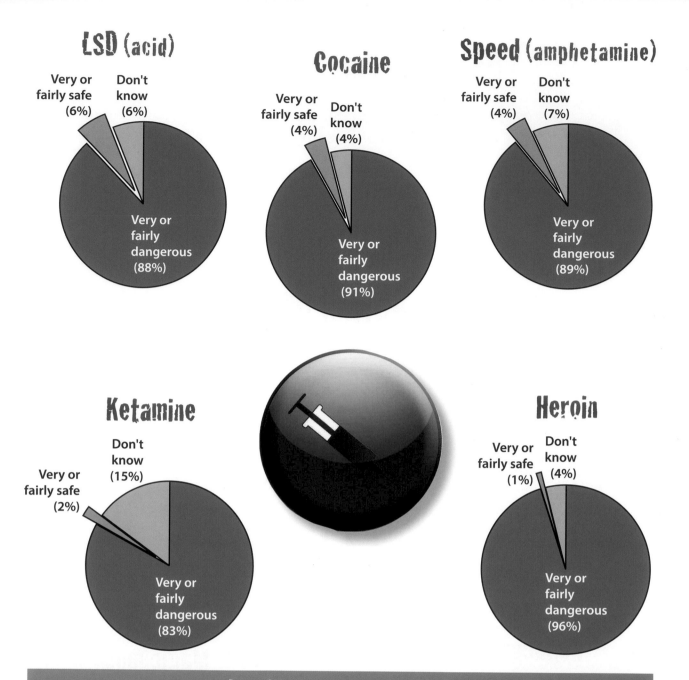

LSD (acid)

Very or fairly safe (6%)

Don't know (6%)

Very or fairly dangerous (88%)

Cocaine

Very or fairly safe (4%)

Don't know (4%)

Very or fairly dangerous (91%)

Speed (amphetamine)

Very or fairly safe (4%)

Don't know (7%)

Very or fairly dangerous (89%)

Ketamine

Don't know (15%)

Very or fairly safe (2%)

Very or fairly dangerous (83%)

Heroin

Very or fairly safe (1%)

Don't know (4%)

Very or fairly dangerous (96%)

Laughing gas – a new high

Laughing gas (Nitrous Oxide) is used in dental procedures and childbirth for pain relief. It has recently become a very popular drug at festivals and concerts because it produces a brief, intense high. It is second only to cannabis as the most popular drug for people aged between 16 and 24.

It is not illegal to possess or use, but it is illegal to sell to anyone under 18 or to drive when under its influence. Some local councils are banning its use because of anti-social behaviour and litter problems.

It carries a relatively low risk but there is some concern that users can suffer oxygen deprivation and loss of blood pressure. It becomes more dangerous when used alongside alcohol.

A random sample of 1,007 of the people in the survey were asked about how SAFE or DANGEROUS they thought laughing gas was:

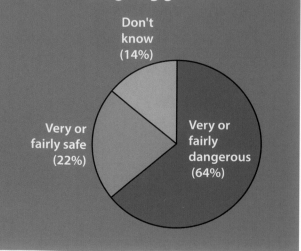

Don't know (14%)

Very or fairly safe (22%)

Very or fairly dangerous (64%)

People thought alcohol was the safest substance. However, a study by the Independent Scientific Committee on Drugs found it was the most harmful.

That study ranked drugs by looking at different measures of ACTUAL harm to users AND to the wider society (ie damage to health, drug dependency, economic costs and crime) and gave them an overall score.

Actual harm

Overall harm score of **selected** drugs
(Drugs were scored out of 100 where 100 = most harmful and 0 = no harm)

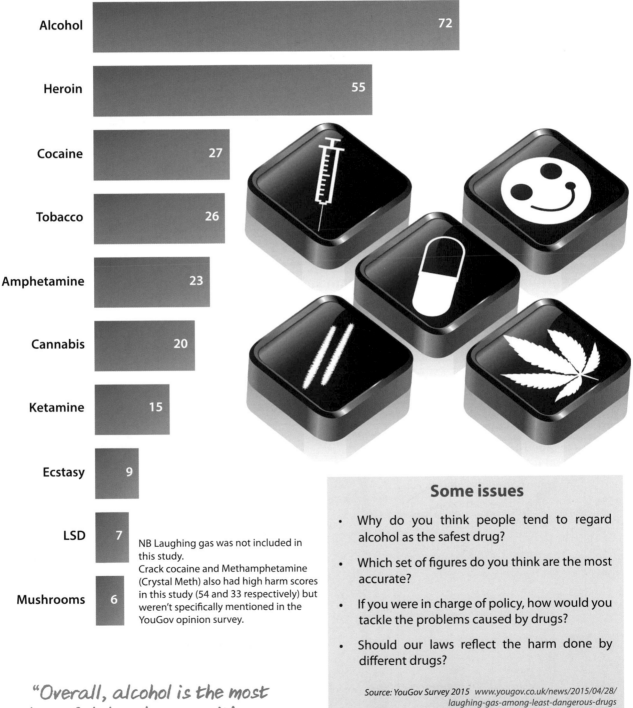

Drug	Score
Alcohol	72
Heroin	55
Cocaine	27
Tobacco	26
Amphetamine	23
Cannabis	20
Ketamine	15
Ecstasy	9
LSD	7
Mushrooms	6

NB Laughing gas was not included in this study.
Crack cocaine and Methamphetamine (Crystal Meth) also had high harm scores in this study (54 and 33 respectively) but weren't specifically mentioned in the YouGov opinion survey.

Some issues

- Why do you think people tend to regard alcohol as the safest drug?

- Which set of figures do you think are the most accurate?

- If you were in charge of policy, how would you tackle the problems caused by drugs?

- Should our laws reflect the harm done by different drugs?

Source: YouGov Survey 2015 www.yougov.co.uk/news/2015/04/28/laughing-gas-among-least-dangerous-drugs

Drug harms in the UK - Professor David Nutt www.thelancet.com

The Week www.theweek.co.uk/legal-highs/54329/hippy-crack-why-nitrous-oxide-is-so-popular-despite-risks

FRANK www.talktofrank.com/drug/nitrous-oxide

"Overall, alcohol is the most harmful drug because it's so widely used."

Prof David J Nutt, former chief drugs adviser to the British government

Getting help: Adult substance misuse

In 2014-15, **295,224** adults (aged over 18) were in contact with drug and alcohol services for treatment for either problematic drug use, alcohol use or both.

The largest group are those who misuse **opiates**. Opiates are painkilling drugs such as codeine, morphine, methadone and diamorphine (heroin). When they are misused, opiates are highly addictive.

Gender split

Men made up **70%** of the total number in treatment in 2014-15.

The gender split varied depending on the substances they were attending for – **73%** of people using drugs were male compared to **62%** with an **alcohol only** problem.

Percentage of clients in treatment by main substance group 2014-15

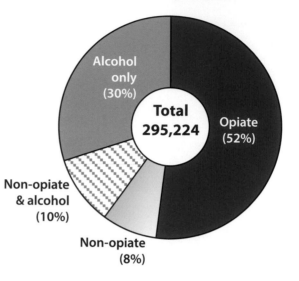

Total 295,224

Alcohol only (30%)
Opiate (52%)
Non-opiate & alcohol (10%)
Non-opiate (8%)

Age groups of all clients and the main substance they were treated for, 2014-15
(Percentages may not add up to 100% due to rounding)

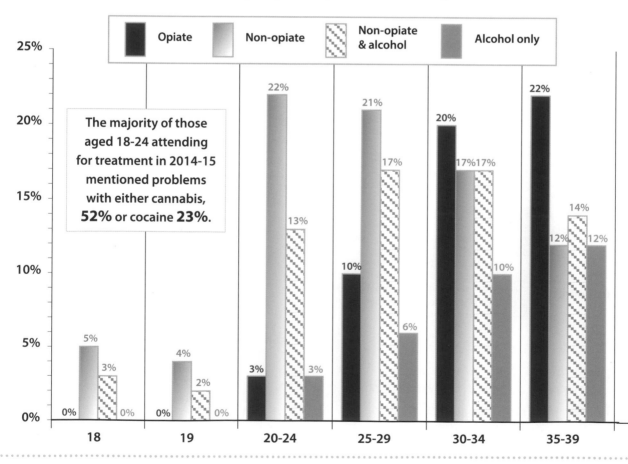

The majority of those aged 18-24 attending for treatment in 2014-15 mentioned problems with either cannabis, **52%** or cocaine **23%**.

Legend: Opiate | Non-opiate | Non-opiate & alcohol | Alcohol only

18: 0%, 5%, 3%, 0%
19: 0%, 4%, 2%, 0%
20-24: 3%, 22%, 13%, 3%
25-29: 10%, 21%, 17%, 6%
30-34: 20%, 17%, 17%, 10%
35-39: 22%, 12%, 14%, 12%

Over ten years the number of people accessing help for substance abuse increased considerably... and the proportion recovering from dependence also increased

The age of people in treatment is rising

Since 2009-10, the number of **opiate** users aged **40 and over** starting treatment has **risen by 21%**.

The overall numbers accessing treatment for **alcohol** have increased by 3%, **but the number** aged 40 and over has **risen by 21%** and the number aged 50 and over by **44%**.

The number of under-25s accessing treatment has fallen by **33%**, with the largest decrease in **opiates** (mainly heroin) where the numbers in treatment have fallen by **60%**.

People are most likely to start using drugs in their late teens and early twenties and, on average, seek treatment within eight years of starting to use them.

The median age* of clients in treatment for each substance group in 2014-15 was:

Opiates	**38 years old**
Non-opiates	29 years old
Non-opiates & alcohol	34 years old
Alcohol only	**45 years old**

Club drugs and new psychoactive substances (NPS) are known as 'legal highs' and are typically used by people in bars and nightclubs, at concerts and parties, before and after a night out.

Most of those accessing treatment for NPS are in the younger age groups, though the total number is relatively low - **1,370** or **0.5%**.

*the middle number in a list of all ages

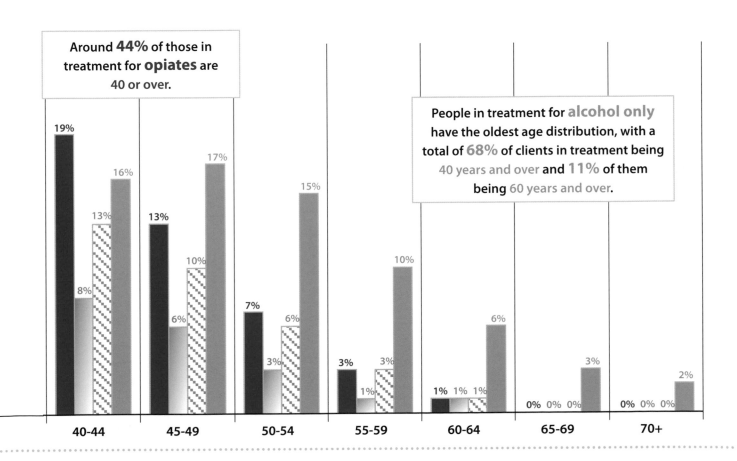

Around **44%** of those in treatment for **opiates** are 40 or over.

People in treatment for alcohol only have the oldest age distribution, with a total of **68%** of clients in treatment being 40 years and over **and 11% of them** being 60 years and over.

40-44: 19%, 8%, 13%, 16%
45-49: 13%, 6%, 10%, 17%
50-54: 7%, 3%, 6%, 15%
55-59: 3%, 1%, 3%, 10%
60-64: 1%, 1%, 1%, 6%
65-69: 0%, 0%, 0%, 3%
70+: 0%, 0%, 0%, 2%

Length of treatment

On average, individuals who completed treatment did so after **334.2** days.

However, the average number of treatment days ranged from **1031.2** days for **opiate** clients to **under 210** days for all the other substance groups.

Leaving treatment

In 2014-15, **130,609** people left the drug and alcohol treatment system.

52% had successfully completed their treatment free of dependence - meaning they had achieved all the care plan goals and were no longer dependent on the substances that bought them into treatment.

27% dropped out or left treatment.

The remaining clients left for other reasons ie transferred to other treatment, transferred into custody, declined treatment etc.

Opiate clients had the highest proportion of incomplete treatment - **38%**.

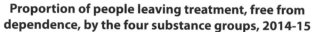

Proportion of people leaving treatment, free from dependence, by the four substance groups, 2014-15

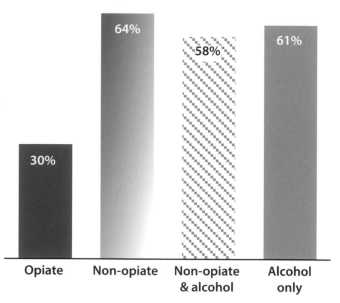

Opiate	Non-opiate	Non-opiate & alcohol	Alcohol only
30%	64%	58%	61%

The recovery rates for non-opiates and alcohol have remained higher and stable mainly because those users are more likely than opiate users to have access to employment and housing.
These personal and social resources can aid recovery.

Helpful organisations

Talk to Frank
www.talktofrank.com

Addaction
www.addaction.org.uk

Adfam
www.adfam.org.uk

Alcohol concern
www.alcoholconcern.org.uk

The Icarus Trust
www.icarustrust.co.uk

Some issues

- Why would opiate users be the largest group in treatment?

- Can you explain the age differences of people in treatment for different substances?

- How do we know when alcohol use becomes problematic? How much is too much?

- What action would you take, if any, to improve the numbers completing their treatment?

Source: Adult substance misuse statistics from the National Drug Treatment Monitoring System (NDTMS) Public Health England © Crown copyright 2015 www.ndtms.net

Alcohol deaths

Rates of alcohol deaths have fallen recently but are still higher at all ages than 20 years ago

The effects of alcohol

Although alcohol is legal for those aged 18 and over, it is still a powerful drug.

Alcohol slows down your body's responses in all kinds of ways. Too much alcohol in a single session could put you in a coma or even kill you.

The human body treats alcohol as a toxic substance - a poison. It removes it by breaking it down in the liver.

Recommended levels

Too much alcohol - binge drinking or regularly drinking above the recommended level - can cause a wide range of health issues such as cancers, heart problems, high blood pressure, stroke, liver disease, and falls and other accidents.

Units of alcohol

Units are a simple way of expressing the quantity of pure alcohol in a drink.

The number of units in a drink is based on the size of the drink as well as its alcohol strength.

One unit equals 10ml or 8g of pure alcohol, which is around the amount of alcohol the average adult can process in an hour. This will vary from person to person.

In January 2016 the government published guidelines, recommending that men and women should drink no more than 14 units of alcohol per week and spread them across several days and have two or three alcohol free days each week.

Unit calculator
(ABV in brackets = the percentage of alcohol in the drink)

Pint of beer, lager or cider:
Regular (4%) **2.3 units**
Strong (5.2%) **3 units**
Extra strong (8%) **4.5 units**

175ml standard glass of wine (13%) **2.3 units**

Single (25ml) measure of spirit & mixer (40%) **1 unit**

275ml bottle of Alcopop (5.5%) **1.5 units**

UK alcohol-related death rates per 100,000, by age and gender 2014

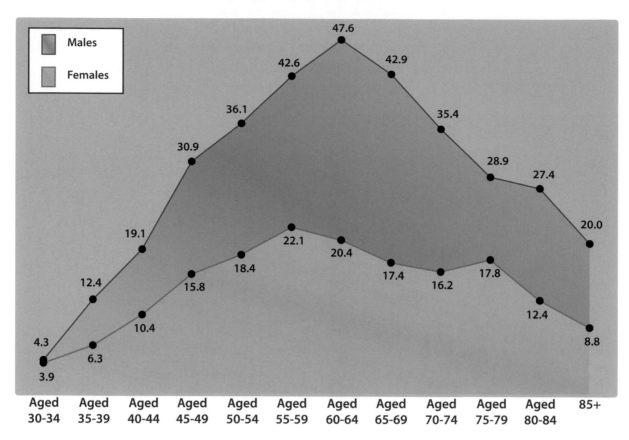

Males
Females

	Aged 30-34	Aged 35-39	Aged 40-44	Aged 45-49	Aged 50-54	Aged 55-59	Aged 60-64	Aged 65-69	Aged 70-74	Aged 75-79	Aged 80-84	85+
Males	4.3	12.4	19.1	30.9	36.1	42.6	47.6	42.9	35.4	28.9	27.4	20.0
Females	3.9	6.3	10.4	15.8	18.4	22.1	20.4	17.4	16.2	17.8	12.4	8.8

NB It is not always possible to calculate reliable age-specific death rates in age groups below 30 to 34 years, because there are generally fewer deaths related to alcohol than at older ages,.

Alcohol-related* deaths in the UK have fallen from **15.8 deaths** per 100,000 people in 2008, when the rate was at its peak, to **14.3 deaths** per 100,000 people in 2014.

UK alcohol-related death rate per 100,000, by gender

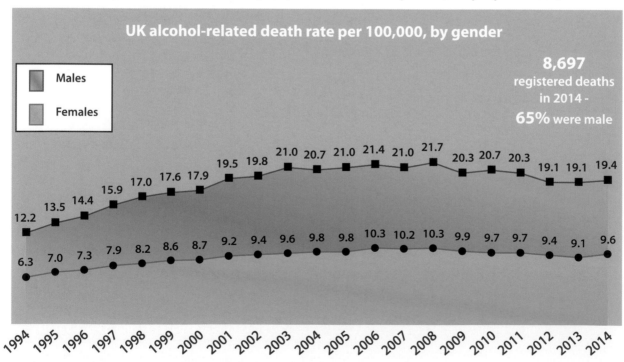

Males
Females

8,697 registered deaths in 2014 - **65%** were male

	1994	1995	1996	1997	1998	1999	2000	2001	2002	2003	2004	2005	2006	2007	2008	2009	2010	2011	2012	2013	2014
Males	12.2	13.5	14.4	15.9	17.0	17.6	17.9	19.5	19.8	21.0	20.7	21.0	21.4	21.0	21.7	20.3	20.7	20.3	19.1	19.1	19.4
Females	6.3	7.0	7.3	7.9	8.2	8.6	8.7	9.2	9.4	9.6	9.8	9.8	10.3	10.2	10.3	9.9	9.7	9.7	9.4	9.1	9.6

*Alcohol-related deaths include underlying causes of death considered as directly due to alcohol consumption - mainly long term abuse but also acute conditions. The figures don't include external causes of death such as road traffic and other accidents or diseases that are partially caused by alcohol.

Deaths where alcohol was recorded as a contributory factor, England & Wales 2014

Underlying cause of death	Proportion of deaths mentioning an alcohol-related condition
Liver cancer	9.9%
Transport accident	5.2%
Cancer of the mouth and throat	2.2%
Hypertensive diseases (heart diseases caused by high blood pressure)	1.4%
Ischaemic heart disease (blocked coronary arteries)	1.0%
Haemorraghic stroke (stroke caused by bleeding in or around the brain)	0.9%
Pneumonia	0.6%
Ischaemic stroke (stroke caused by a blood clot)	0.5%
Cancer of the oesophagus	0.4%

10.8 million
adults in England are **drinking at levels**
that pose some risk to their health

1.6 million adults may have some
level of alcohol dependence

Helpful organisations

Alcohol concern
www.alcoholconcern.org.uk

Talk to Frank
www.talktofrank.com/drug/alcohol

Drinkaware
www.drinkaware.co.uk

Al-Anon
www.al-anonuk.org.uk

Drinkline
Helpline: 0300 123 1110

Some issues

- Why do people continue to drink too much despite the health risks?

- What reasons could there be for alcohol related deaths increasing or declining?

- Why is drinking alcohol so socially acceptable when it is so damaging to our health?

- Should the NHS provide free treatment for people who have caused their own illness?

Source: Alcohol-related deaths in the UK, Office for National Statistics www.ons.gov.uk Health matters: harmful drinking and alcohol dependence © Crown copyright 2016 www.gov.uk NHS Choices www.nhs.uk/Livewell/alcohol/Pages/alcohol-units.aspx Change4Life www.nhs.uk/change4life/Pages/alcohol-lower-risk-guidelines-units.aspx

Quitting smoking

Are e-cigarettes the answer?

Smoking among adults and young people has fallen dramatically. **19% of adults** in Great Britain currently **smoke**, down from a peak of **46%** in 1974.

The average number of cigarettes smoked peaked in 1976 at **16.8** cigarettes per person, per day.

This is now down to **11.4** cigarettes a day – the lowest number recorded.

Smoking remains the main cause of preventable death in Great Britain, but many people who wish to stop smoking find it hard. Using e-cigarettes (vaping) may help them to quit.

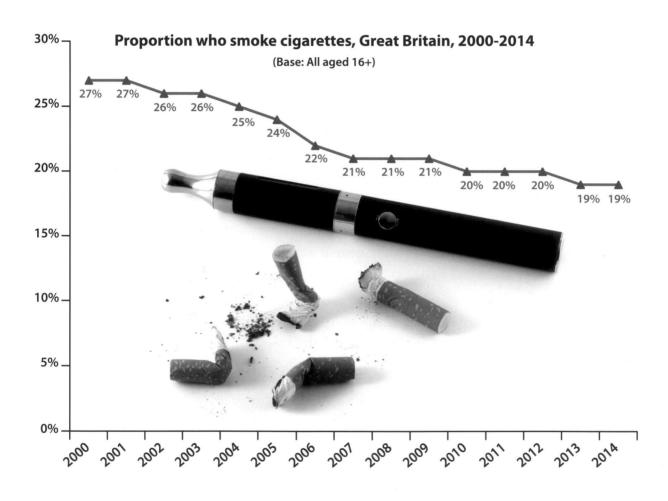

Proportion who smoke cigarettes, Great Britain, 2000-2014
(Base: All aged 16+)

Year	Percentage
2000	27%
2001	27%
2002	26%
2003	26%
2004	25%
2005	24%
2006	22%
2007	21%
2008	21%
2009	21%
2010	20%
2011	20%
2012	20%
2013	19%
2014	19%

Why is it hard to stop smoking?

The reason that smoking is hard to quit is that nicotine is addictive and quitting is uncomfortable and difficult. But it is not nicotine which causes most of the health problems for smokers - it is burning tobacco that does the damage to smokers' health.

How do e-cigarettes work?

e-cigarettes use battery power to heat an element which makes vapour from a liquid containing nicotine.

They do not contain tobacco, do not create smoke and do not rely on burning - so there is much less risk to health.

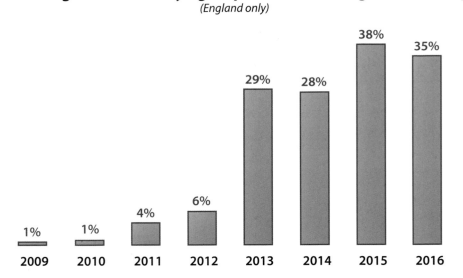

Percentage of smokers trying to quit who used e-cigarettes to help
(England only)

Year	Percentage
2009	1%
2010	1%
2011	4%
2012	6%
2013	29%
2014	28%
2015	38%
2016	35%

An 'Action on Smoking and Health' (ASH) Survey in 2015 confirmed that ex-smokers in Great Britain found e-cigarettes an aid to quitting

I use/used electronic cigarettes...	Smokers	Ex-smokers
Just to give it a try	35%	29%
To help me stop smoking tobacco entirely	30%	44%
To help me reduce the amount of tobacco I smoke, but not stop completely	29%	9%
Because I had made an attempt to quit smoking already and I wanted an aid to help me keep off tobacco	27%	35%
To save money compared with smoking tobacco	24%	22%
Because I felt I was addicted to smoking tobacco and could not stop using it even though I wanted to	16%	17%
Because I want to continue to smoke tobacco and I needed something to help deal with situations where I cannot smoke (eg workplaces, bars or restaurants)	15%	8%
To avoid putting those around me at risk due to second-hand tobacco smoke	12%	13%
Other	1%	3%

Are e-cigarettes safe?

Although no one can say they are 100% safe, experts estimate that e-cigarettes are around 95% safer than smoking.

They do not contain most of the chemicals which cause diseases in smokers and the chemicals they do contain only pose a limited threat to health.

Since it is so hard to stamp out the addiction, it is better to make nicotine safer to use.

Some issues

- Vaping (using e-cigarettes) is safer than smoking. But should health services really try to solve the addiction problem?

- Vaping is banned in many public places because it makes smoking appear normal - instead of something forbidden. Is this a good policy?

- Could vaping promote nicotine addiction in young people?

Source: Adult smoking habits in Great Britain - Office for National Statistics © Crown copyright 2016 www.ons.gov.uk Trends in electronic cigarette use in England www.smokinginengland.info E-cigarettes: an evidence update www.gov.uk

Getting help: Young people & drugs

Alcohol and drug problems in young people seem to be declining but some still need help

Specialist substance misuse services support young people who are experiencing harm from their alcohol and drug use to prevent it from becoming a greater problem as they get older.

During 2014-15 there were **18,349** young people aged 9-17 in contact with treatment services - a **decrease of 4%** over the previous year.

The majority of young people in treatment have a range of problems related to their substance use. Girls are more likely to report mental health problems and self-harming while boys are more likely to be involved in antisocial behaviour and not be in education, employment or training (NEET).

Under 18s receiving treatment, by age group

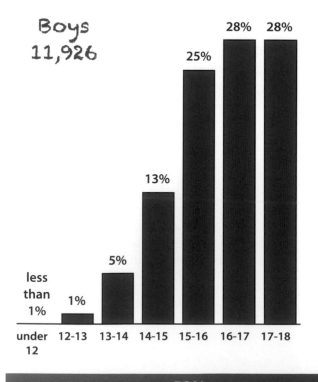

Boys
11,926

under 12	12-13	13-14	14-15	15-16	16-17	17-18
less than 1%	1%	5%	13%	25%	28%	28%

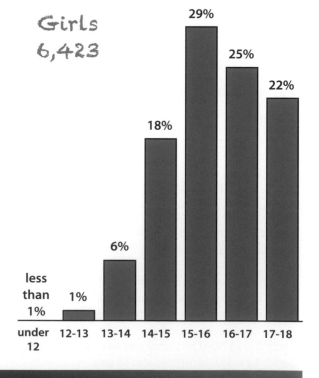

Girls
6,423

under 12	12-13	13-14	14-15	15-16	16-17	17-18
less than 1%	1%	6%	18%	29%	25%	22%

52% of all the young people were aged 16 or over.

65% of young people accessing treatment were male.

25% of the girls in treatment were under 15, compared to **19%** of boys.

Percentage of young people under 18 in treatment, by primary substance (the one which brought them into treatment) and additional substances mentioned, 2014-15

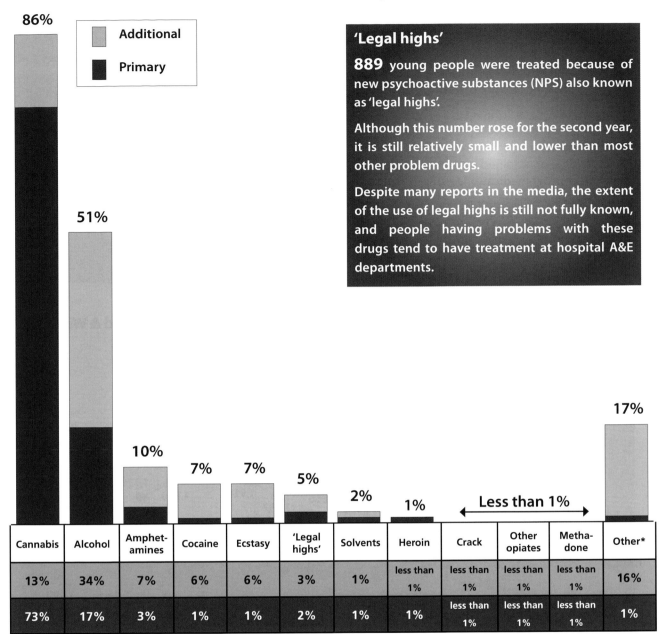

Legend:
- Additional (light grey)
- Primary (black)

Bar values: Cannabis 86%, Alcohol 51%, Amphetamines 10%, Cocaine 7%, Ecstasy 7%, 'Legal highs' 5%, Solvents 2%, Heroin 1%, Crack–Methadone: Less than 1%, Other* 17%

	Cannabis	Alcohol	Amphet-amines	Cocaine	Ecstasy	'Legal highs'	Solvents	Heroin	Crack	Other opiates	Metha-done	Other*
	13%	34%	7%	6%	6%	3%	1%	less than 1%	less than 1%	less than 1%	less than 1%	16%
	73%	17%	3%	1%	1%	2%	1%	1%	less than 1%	less than 1%	less than 1%	1%

*Substance categories not shown elsewhere

Some helpful organisations

Adfam
www.adfam.org.uk

Families Anonymous
www.famanon.org.uk

Frank
www.talktofrank.com

Hope UK
www.hopeuk.org

The Site
www.thesite.org

Some issues

- Why, in your opinion, is there is such a difference in the figures for boys and girls?

- Do the numbers of young people getting treatment seem large to you?

- Are young people sufficiently aware of the possible problems associated with drug use?

Source: Young people's statistics from the National Drug Treatment Monitoring System, Public Health England © Crown copyright 2015
www.nta.nhs.uk/statistics.aspx

Amphetamine-type stimulants (ATS) and new psychoactive substances (NPS)

Amphetamines remain the second most commonly used drug after cannabis. ATS are synthetic drugs that could potentially be manufactured anywhere - unlike heroin and cocaine, they do not depend on plants that have to be cultivated and need certain conditions to grow.

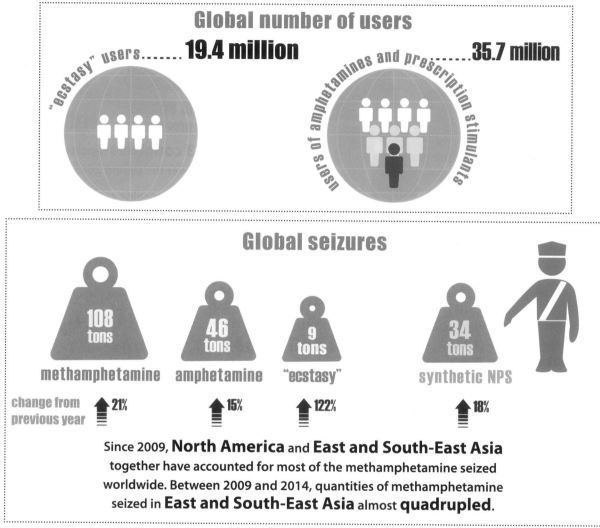

Global number of users

"ecstasy" users....... **19.4 million**

users of amphetamines and prescription stimulants .... **35.7 million**

Global seizures

108 tons methamphetamine	46 tons amphetamine	9 tons "ecstasy"	34 tons synthetic NPS
change from previous year ▲ 21%	▲ 15%	▲ 122%	▲ 18%

Since 2009, **North America** and **East and South-East Asia** together have accounted for most of the methamphetamine seized worldwide. Between 2009 and 2014, quantities of methamphetamine seized in **East and South-East Asia** almost **quadrupled**.

Note: Amphetamines include both amphetamine and methampetamine. Seizures of synthetic NPS do not include seizures of plant-based substances and ketamine.
NB Latest available figures 2014

New psychoactive substances

Between 2008 and the end of 2015, a total of **644** NPS were reported by 102 countries and territories - the majority were in Europe (41), followed by Asia (30), Africa (16), the Americas (13) and Oceania (2).

NPS were reported for the first time in 2015 in Kyrgyzstan and Mauritius.

The NPS market continues to grow with a large number of new substances being reported. Before the end of 2015 at least **75** new substances had been reported to the United Nations Office on Drugs and Crime for the first time.

Some issues

- Why is the drugs trade such a cause for concern?

- Would there be fewer or more problems if the use of drugs was legalised?

- What should be done to avoid the health problems associated with drugs?

Source: United Nations Office on Drugs and Crime, World Drug Report 2016 © United Nations, May 2016
www.unodc.org

Animals

Animal research: Facts and figures

The facts

Why do we need animals in research?

Humans share at least 90% of their genes with every other mammal, and have the same vital organs, ie heart, lungs, liver, kidneys and brain.

The law says that animals cannot be used if medical research or testing can be done by a non-animal method but all potential medicines for humans must be safety-tested on animals first.

Does it work?

Animal research has been used to control diabetes, asthma and high blood pressure and has been used to develop antibiotics, vaccines, anaesthetics and blood transfusions.

But animals may respond to a drug differently to a human which can cause stress to the animal and affect the test result.

What is a procedure?

A procedure can be defined as: *any act carried out on an animal that may cause it a level of pain, suffering or distress equivalent to or greater than injecting it with a hypodermic needle.*

The number of procedures, is usually the same as the number of animals used. Sometimes animals are 'reused' when they have fully recovered from a previous procedure and then counted again.

The figures here all relate to the number of procedures, not the number of animals.

Does it hurt the animals?

Lab animals are protected from cruelty during procedures by law. All labs have regular inspections to make sure that testing is being carried out properly.

What are the alternatives?

- Taking tissue samples from humans and testing the drugs on them in a test tube.

- Carrying out experiments using computer models and programmes.

- Looking at large numbers of statistics.

The figures

4.14 million procedures were carried out on animals in Great Britain in 2015.

Around half of these, **2.08 million,** were **experimental procedures.**

Experimental procedures are used for basic research purposes, research on humans and animals, procedures to ensure the safety and effectiveness of pharmaceuticals eg quality control of marketed medicines and procedures to satisfy legal requirements.

The remaining **2.06 million** procedures were for the creation/breeding of genetically altered animals but not used in further procedures.

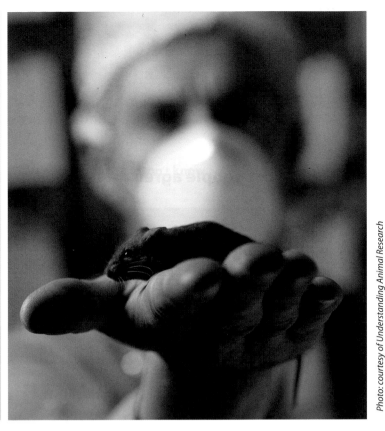

Photo: courtesy of Understanding Animal Research

Species of animal used in each experimental procedure, 2015

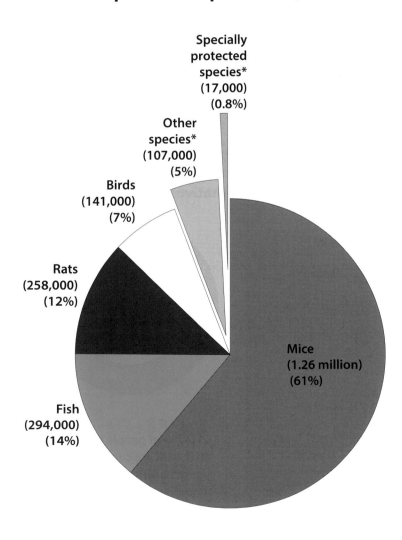

Specially protected species* (17,000) (0.8%)

Other species* (107,000) (5%)

Birds (141,000) (7%)

Rats (258,000) (12%)

Fish (294,000) (14%)

Mice (1.26 million) (61%)

*Other species include guinea pigs, hamsters, gerbils, rabbits, ferrets, pigs, goats, sheep, cattle, reptiles, amphibians etc.

Specially protected species include horses/donkeys, dogs, cats, and non-human primates.

NB Figures may not add up to 100% due to rounding

Main ways in which dogs were reunited with their owners

(Base: 349 GB authorities)

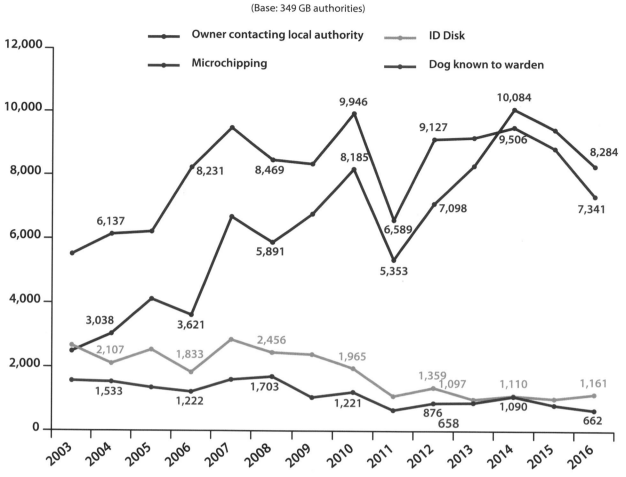

- Owner contacting local authority
- Microchipping
- ID Disk
- Dog known to warden

	2003	2004	2005	2006	2007	2008	2009	2010	2011	2012	2013	2014	2015	2016
Dog known to warden		6,137		8,231		8,469		9,946	6,589	9,127		10,084		8,284
Microchipping						5,891		8,185	5,353	7,098		9,506		7,341
ID Disk	2,107		1,833		2,456		1,965			1,359 / 1,097	1,110		1,161
Owner contacting local authority	3,038		3,621		1,703		1,221		876 / 658		1,090		662
ID Disk start	1,533		1,222											

MISSING

REWARD FOR SAFE RETURN

Figures from Dogs Trust also show that traditional means of trying to find a missing dog are largely ineffective. **50%** of those surveyed said when they see a missing dog poster, they never take any action to note down the contact information or details.

Some issues

- Should there be some restriction on who can own a dog?

- What would be the best way to find a missing dog?

- Will microchipping all dogs solve the problem with strays?

- If a stray is rehomed and the original owner wants it back, what should be done?

Base: 2016 Stray Dog Survey by GfK NOP and a separate survey of 1,000 UK-based dog owners was carried out by OnePoll on behalf of the Dogs Trust. *Source: Dogs Trust www.dogstrust.org.uk*

Britain & its citizens

Snap judgements

How we regard people - before we have even met

A YouGov survey looked at the sort of **judgements** we often make about strangers based on their age, gender and ethnic group.

They asked questions about eight ethnic/national or religious groups: White; Black Caribbean; White Australian Pakistani; Polish; Muslim; Chinese; and Jewish

Three age groups: 20s, 40s and 60s **and two genders.**

This gave 48 possible groupings.

The questions were:

How likely is each group to possess these positive qualities?

Be intelligent

Be honest

Work hard

Be polite

Help others

How likely is each group to possess these **negative qualities?**

Be violent

Travel without buying a ticket

Take drugs

Have many sexual partners

Get drunk frequently

For each group the score for all the negative qualities was subtracted from the total score for positive qualities to give an overall ranking.

The **pre-judgement** this revealed was clear:

"The people we regard as the laziest, rudest, most promiscuous, drunken drug-takers are white men in their twenties."

White men in their 20s were the most derided and looked down on.

They were seen as the least likely to be polite and the second least likely to work hard or to help others. They were viewed as the most likely to take drugs, to have many sexual partners and to get drunk frequently.

In contrast, white women in their 60s were praised as most honest, polite and helpful. They were also least likely to be violent.

Overall six most praised groups
(score)

Group	Score
White woman in her 60s	67
White man in his 60s	64
Chinese woman in her 40s	61
Chinese woman in her 60s	60
Jewish woman in her 40s	59
Jewish man in his 60s	59

Overall six most derided groups
(score)

Group	Score
White man in his 20s	8
Black Caribbean man in his 20s	19
White woman in her 20s	23
White Australian man in his 20s	27
Pakistani-born man in his 20s	28
Polish-born man in his 20s	28

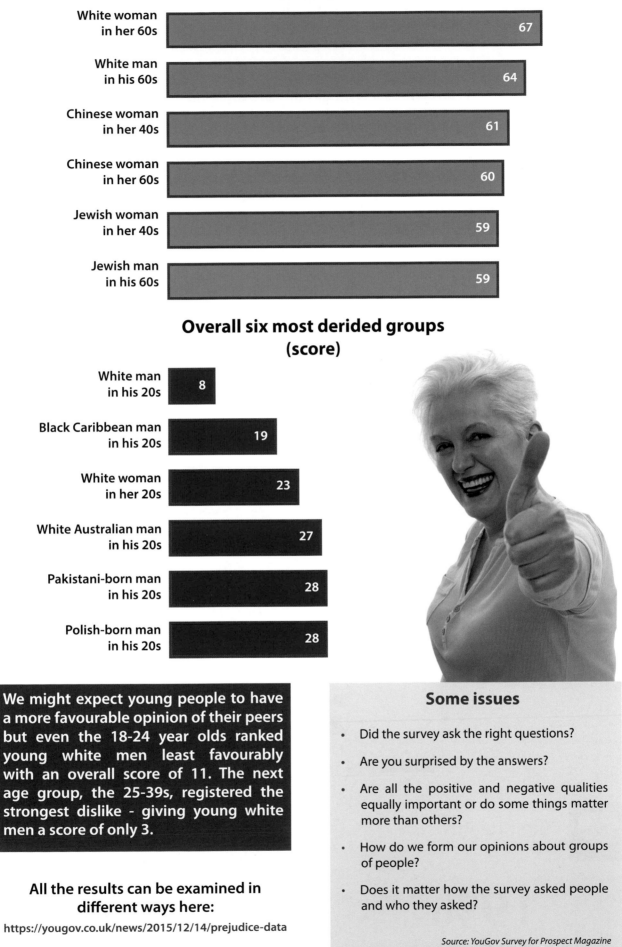

We might expect young people to have a more favourable opinion of their peers but even the 18-24 year olds ranked young white men least favourably with an overall score of 11. The next age group, the 25-39s, registered the strongest dislike - giving young white men a score of only 3.

All the results can be examined in different ways here:

https://yougov.co.uk/news/2015/12/14/prejudice-data

NB YouGov did not give a base for the data

Some issues

- Did the survey ask the right questions?

- Are you surprised by the answers?

- Are all the positive and negative qualities equally important or do some things matter more than others?

- How do we form our opinions about groups of people?

- Does it matter how the survey asked people and who they asked?

Source: YouGov Survey for Prospect Magazine
https://yougov.co.uk/news/2015/12/14/young-white-men-most-derided

Major causes of stress

What worries people in the UK?

In an online survey, 1,501 British people aged 15+ were asked what were major causes of stress in their lives.

(More than one answer could be given and percentages are rounded)

Top 5 major causes of stress

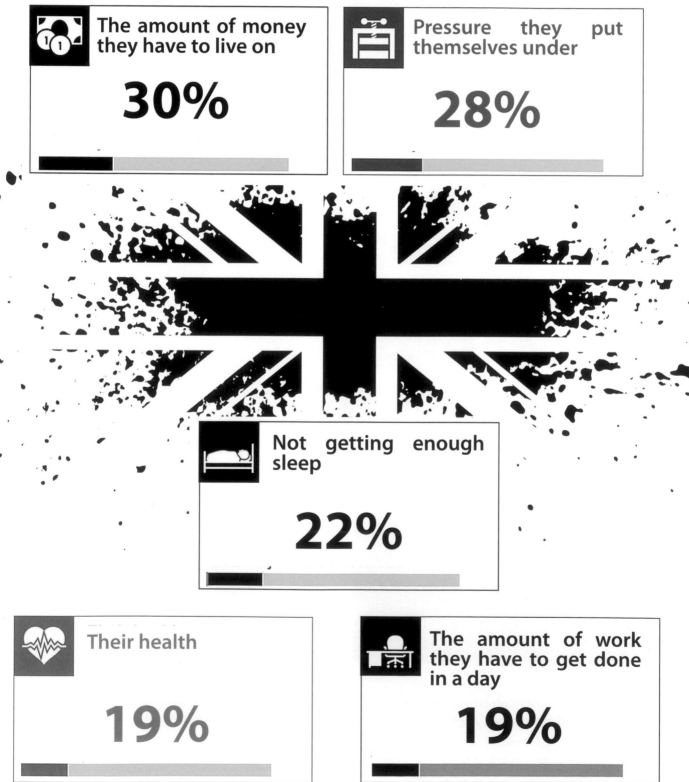

The amount of money they have to live on

30%

Pressure they put themselves under

28%

Not getting enough sleep

22%

Their health

19%

The amount of work they have to get done in a day

19%

Top 5 major causes of stress for women

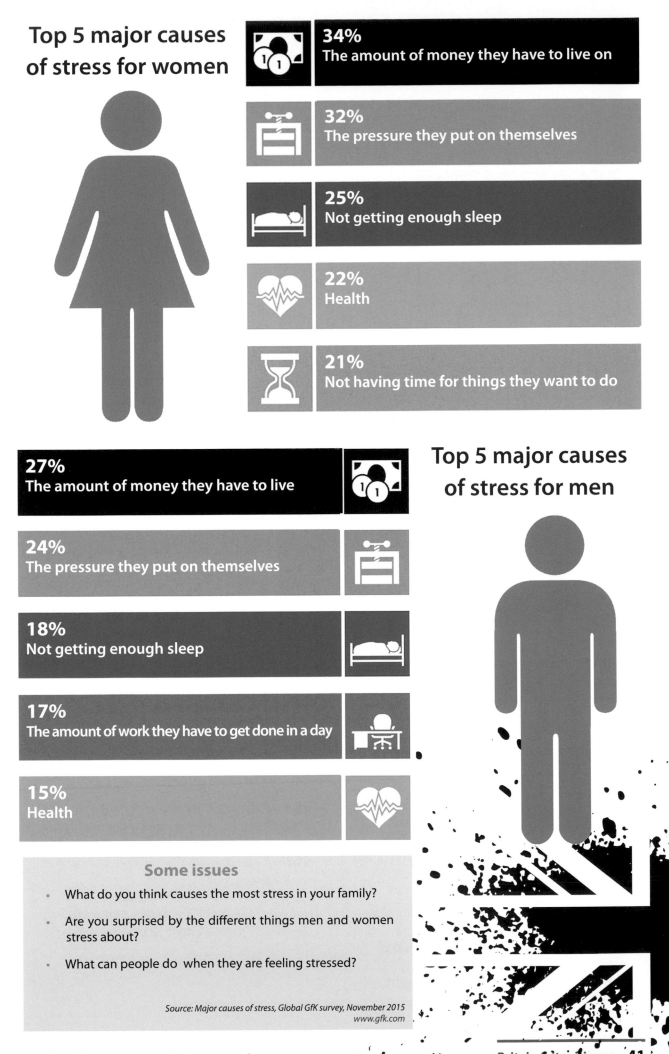

34% The amount of money they have to live on

32% The pressure they put on themselves

25% Not getting enough sleep

22% Health

21% Not having time for things they want to do

Top 5 major causes of stress for men

27% The amount of money they have to live

24% The pressure they put on themselves

18% Not getting enough sleep

17% The amount of work they have to get done in a day

15% Health

Some issues

- What do you think causes the most stress in your family?
- Are you surprised by the different things men and women stress about?
- What can people do when they are feeling stressed?

Source: Major causes of stress, Global GfK survey, November 2015
www.gfk.com

Human rights matter

Which are most important to British adults?

Which rights matter most?

Over 9,000 adults in 8 countries, in Europe and the USA, were shown a selection of **30 rights** chosen from United Nations and European Council declarations and the British and American Bills of Rights.

They could select up to **10 rights** from the 30, as the most important.

To make it easier to choose, the 30 rights were divided into two lists of 15 each and people selected **four or five from each list**.

Finally they chose **the one right** they considered as the most important of all.

The figures here focus on the views of 1,700 adults in Great Britain.

Other countries in the survey sometimes chose different rights as the most important, for example, the right to own a gun was selected by **46%** of Americans but by no more than **6%** in any European country.

However, the right to **free speech** was selected by **more than 50%** of people in all the countries.

The rights British people chose as MOST important
(List 1)

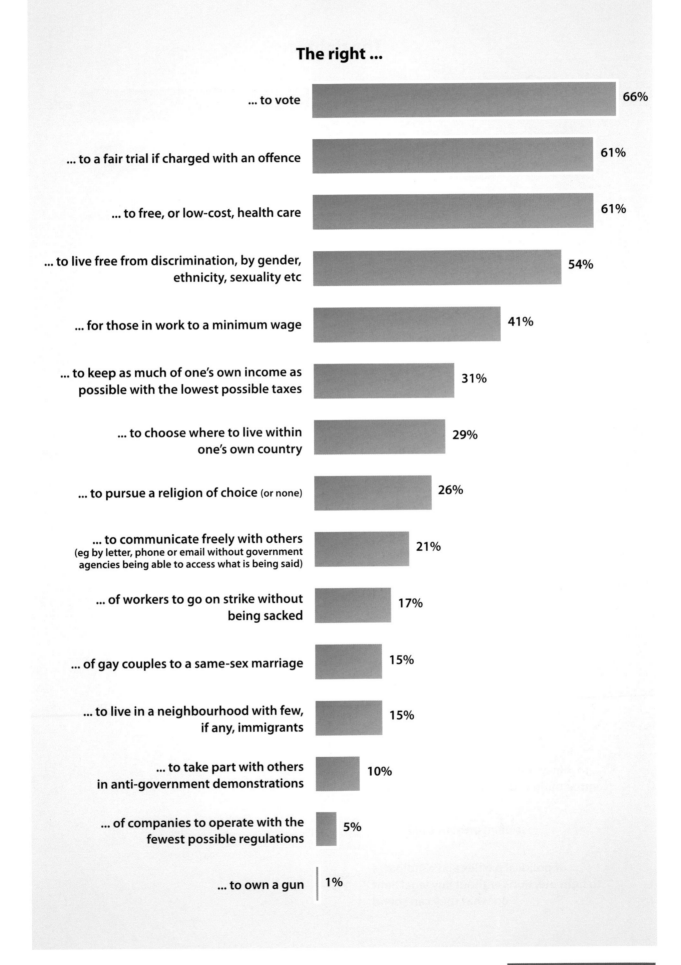

The right ...

... to vote	66%
... to a fair trial if charged with an offence	61%
... to free, or low-cost, health care	61%
... to live free from discrimination, by gender, ethnicity, sexuality etc	54%
... for those in work to a minimum wage	41%
... to keep as much of one's own income as possible with the lowest possible taxes	31%
... to choose where to live within one's own country	29%
... to pursue a religion of choice (or none)	26%
... to communicate freely with others (eg by letter, phone or email without government agencies being able to access what is being said)	21%
... of workers to go on strike without being sacked	17%
... of gay couples to a same-sex marriage	15%
... to live in a neighbourhood with few, if any, immigrants	15%
... to take part with others in anti-government demonstrations	10%
... of companies to operate with the fewest possible regulations	5%
... to own a gun	1%

The rights British people chose as MOST important
(List 2)

The right ...

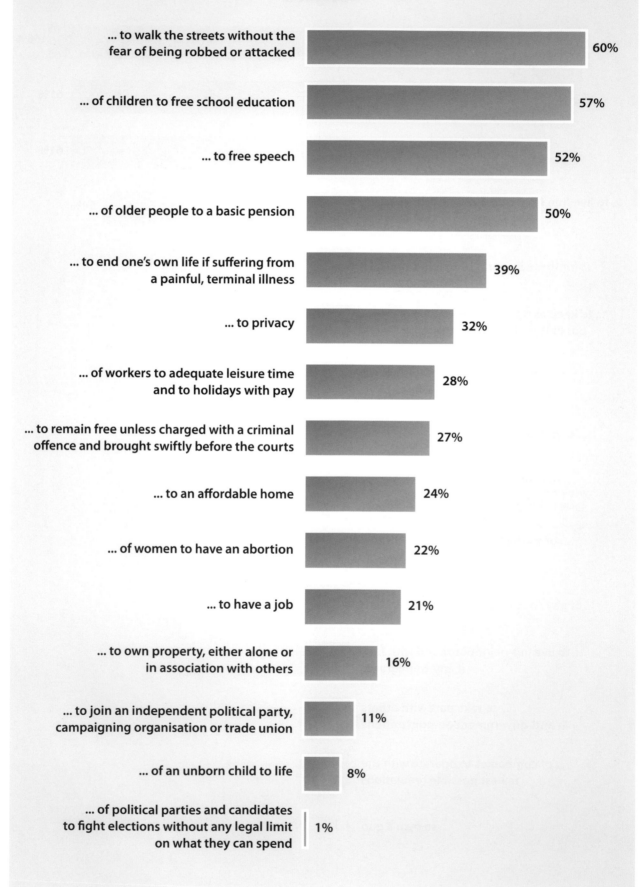

The right ...	%
... to walk the streets without the fear of being robbed or attacked	60%
... of children to free school education	57%
... to free speech	52%
... of older people to a basic pension	50%
... to end one's own life if suffering from a painful, terminal illness	39%
... to privacy	32%
... of workers to adequate leisure time and to holidays with pay	28%
... to remain free unless charged with a criminal offence and brought swiftly before the courts	27%
... to an affordable home	24%
... of women to have an abortion	22%
... to have a job	21%
... to own property, either alone or in association with others	16%
... to join an independent political party, campaigning organisation or trade union	11%
... of an unborn child to life	8%
... of political parties and candidates to fight elections without any legal limit on what they can spend	1%

Which ONE of the 10 rights they had chosen was the MOST important?

(**NB** Some rights have been abbreviated
Figures do not add up to 100% due to rounding)

The right ...

... to a minimum wage **2%**

... to an affordable home **2%**

... to have a job **2%**

... to pursue a religion 1%

... to a same-sex marriage 1%

... to communicate freely with others 1%

... of an unborn child to life 1%

... of workers to leisure time and paid holidays 1%

... to remain free unless charged with a criminal offence... **3%**

... to privacy **3%**

... to keep as much of one's own income as possible ... **3%**

... to live in a neighbourhood with few, if any, immigrants **3%**

... to a fair trial ... **3%**

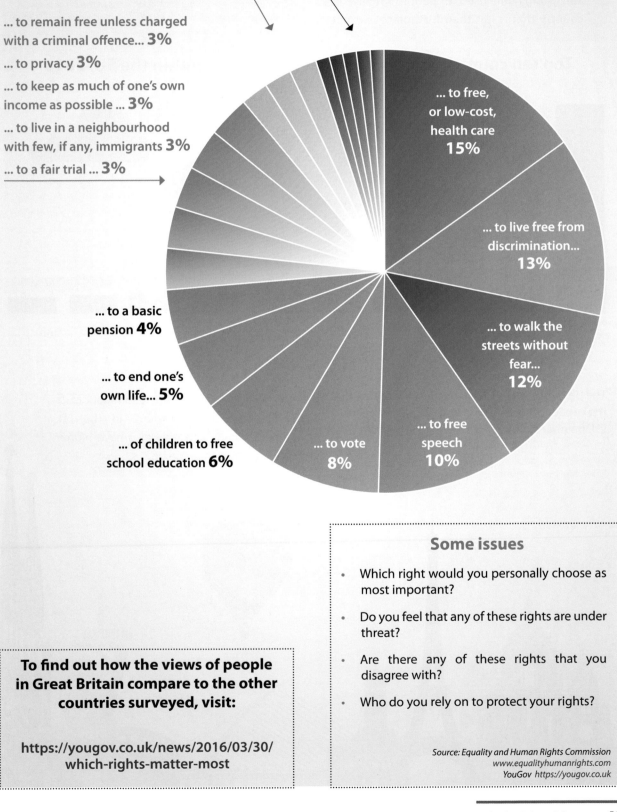

... to free, or low-cost, health care **15%**

... to live free from discrimination... **13%**

... to walk the streets without fear... **12%**

... to a basic pension **4%**

... to end one's own life... **5%**

... of children to free school education **6%**

... to vote **8%**

... to free speech **10%**

Some issues

- Which right would you personally choose as most important?

- Do you feel that any of these rights are under threat?

- Are there any of these rights that you disagree with?

- Who do you rely on to protect your rights?

To find out how the views of people in Great Britain compare to the other countries surveyed, visit:

https://yougov.co.uk/news/2016/03/30/which-rights-matter-most

Source: Equality and Human Rights Commission
www.equalityhumanrights.com
YouGov https://yougov.co.uk

Expats

People who choose to live in foreign countries

While EU immigration into Britain continues to rise, there are also **1.2 million** people born in the UK who live in other European countries, according to 2015 data from the United Nations.

The group name used for people who live in a country that is not their birthplace is expats, short for expatriates, which simply means 'out of country'.

After the Brexit* vote it seems likely that both their status and the status of EU nationals living in the UK could change.

* The vote to choose whether the UK stays in the EU or not, the outcome of which was that the UK should leave the EU.

Top ten countries UK citizens have moved to within the EU, 2015

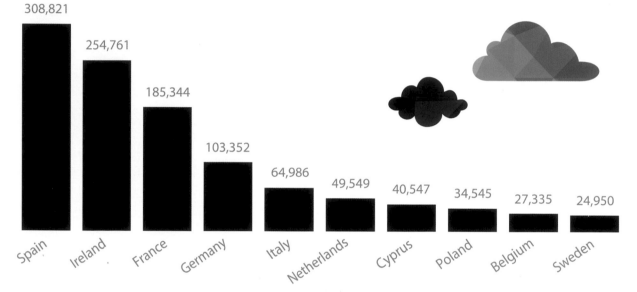

Spain	308,821
Ireland	254,761
France	185,344
Germany	103,352
Italy	64,986
Netherlands	49,549
Cyprus	40,547
Poland	34,545
Belgium	27,335
Sweden	24,950

The UK is fifth among EU countries for the size of the expat population who have moved to other EU member countries.

Poland has the most: an estimated **3.5 million** Poles live elsewhere in the EU. Romania, Germany and Italy also have higher expat populations than the UK.

All long-term immigration in the EU
(2014)

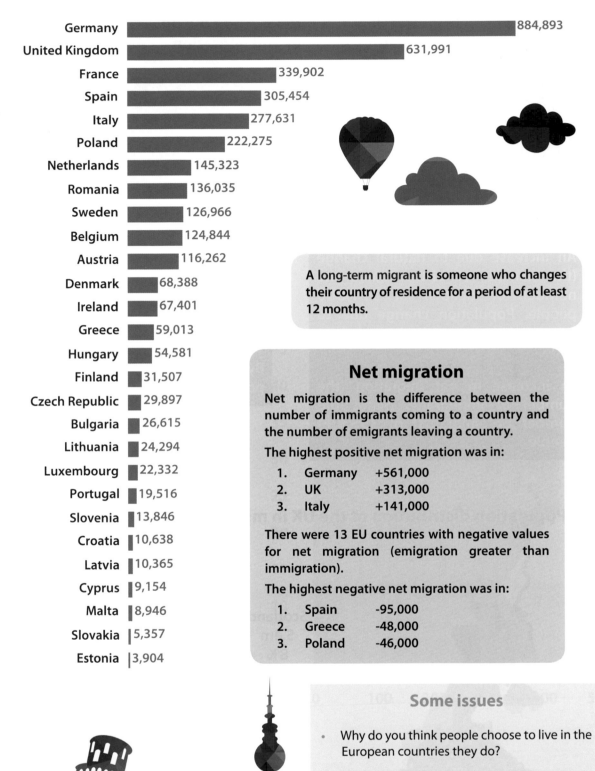

Germany	884,893
United Kingdom	631,991
France	339,902
Spain	305,454
Italy	277,631
Poland	222,275
Netherlands	145,323
Romania	136,035
Sweden	126,966
Belgium	124,844
Austria	116,262
Denmark	68,388
Ireland	67,401
Greece	59,013
Hungary	54,581
Finland	31,507
Czech Republic	29,897
Bulgaria	26,615
Lithuania	24,294
Luxembourg	22,332
Portugal	19,516
Slovenia	13,846
Croatia	10,638
Latvia	10,365
Cyprus	9,154
Malta	8,946
Slovakia	5,357
Estonia	3,904

A long-term migrant is someone who changes their country of residence for a period of at least 12 months.

Net migration

Net migration is the difference between the number of immigrants coming to a country and the number of emigrants leaving a country.

The highest positive net migration was in:

1. Germany   +561,000
2. UK   +313,000
3. Italy   +141,000

There were 13 EU countries with negative values for net migration (emigration greater than immigration).

The highest negative net migration was in:

1. Spain   -95,000
2. Greece   -48,000
3. Poland   -46,000

Some issues

- Why do you think people choose to live in the European countries they do?

- Would you ever want to move abroad and why? Which country would you choose?

- What would you miss most about life in this country and what would you miss least?

Source: Trends in international migrant stock, United Nations
un.org/en,
Brits abroad: how many people from the UK live in other EU countries?
fullfact.org
UK Perspectives 2016: The UK in a European context, visual.ons.gov.uk
Eurostat ec.europa.eu/eurostat

UK population continues to age

There are now **over 11.6 million** people (**17.8%** of the population) aged **65 and over** and **1.5 million** (**2.3%** of the population) **aged 85 and over**.

Since 2005, the UK population **aged 65 and over** has increased by **21%**, and the population **aged 85 and over** has increased by **31%**.

The number of **males aged 85 and over** has increased by **54%**, compared to a **21%** increase for **females**.

How does the population differ across the UK?

Natural change

London had the **largest** natural change of all regions with **78,400 more births than deaths**.

North East of England the **smallest**, with **100 more deaths than births** - the first time since mid-2005 the number of deaths has exceeded the number of births in an English region.

All regions experienced an increase in the number of deaths in the year to mid-2015.

Migration

London was the destination of **38%** of international migrants arriving in England and Wales, giving it the highest net international migration of all regions at **133,900** – up by **26,500** from the previous year.

Wales had the lowest net international migration with **5,900** more people arriving to stay from abroad than emigrating.

The **South West of England** received more people from other parts of the UK than any other region, leading to a **29,600** population increase.

London had the greatest outflow of people to other parts of the UK of any region, with a net loss of **77,500** people.

More people of every age left London for other parts of the UK than arrived, except for people aged 21-28, more of whom arrived.

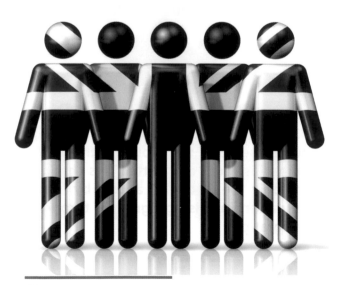

Some issues

- Is population growth a good thing? Can it be a bad thing?

- Why do some people have such strong views about population growth?

- How might an ageing population affect you and your age group?

- Why do you think many 21-28 year olds want to live in London?

Source: Population Estimates for UK, England and Wales, Scotland and Northern Ireland mid-2015; National Population Projections: 2014, Office for National Statistics © Crown copyright 2016 https://www.ons.gov.uk

Disability

Disability UK

A snapshot of what life is like for people with a disability

What is disability?

A person has a disability if they have a physical or mental difficulty which has a substantial and long term effect on **normal day to day activities**.

Almost **1 in 5** people (**19%**) have a disability in the UK, that's around **11.9 million** disabled people.

The most common problems are:

- mobility - difficulty with movement and walking **57%**
- stamina/breathing/ fatigue **38%**
- dexterity - being able to handle things easily **28%**
- mental health **16%**

Often people have more than one impairment.

Most impairments are not immediately visible, eg there are only **1.2 million wheelchair users** in the UK.

Education

11% of people without a disability have no formal qualifications compared to **30%** of disabled adults.

28% of disabled 19 year olds are not in any form of education, employment or training (NEET) compared to **13%** of those without a disability.

Age

Only **17%** of disabled people were born with their disabilities. Disability becomes more common as we get older.

- **7%** of children are disabled
- **16%** of adults of working age
- **43%** of adults over state pension age
- **67%** of those aged **75 and over** have a long-standing illness or disability, compared with **14%** of those aged 16–24.

Children

0.9 million children under the age of 16 in the UK are disabled - the fastest growing group among the population of disabled people.

For disabled children, the most common impairments are:

- social and behavioural 33%

- learning disability 31%

- stamina, breathing and fatigue 31%

Boys have a higher rate of disability than girls, and are more likely to experience social and behavioural, learning and memory difficulties.

It is estimated that the proportion of children and young people who are disabled will increase and that there will be over 1.25 million children reporting a disability by 2029.

The reasons include:

- improved diagnosis;

- reduced stigma in reporting disability; and

- better survival rates for pre-term infants.

It is estimated that there will be 450,000 children and young people (aged 0–19) with learning disabilities in the UK by 2031.

The annual cost of bringing up a disabled child is three times greater than that of bringing up a non-disabled child.

40% of disabled children in the UK live in poverty. This is around 320,000 disabled children, and almost a third of those are classified as living in 'severe poverty'.

There is a 2 way relationship between disability and poverty in childhood: Disabled children are amongst the most likely to experience poverty, and children from poorer backgrounds are more likely to become disabled than those who are better off.

Cost of living

Disabled people's day to day living costs – for basics like mobility aids, care and transport – are **25% higher** than those of people who do not have a disability.

Disabled people pay on average **£550 per month** in extra costs related to their disability.

They are **3 times** more likely to use doorstep **loans**, and have on average **£108,000 fewer savings and assets** than non-disabled people.

Half of disabled people have used a **credit card or loan** to pay for **everyday items**, such as clothing or food.

33% of households with a disabled person could not afford to pay for a week's annual holiday away from home, compared with **20%** of households without a disabled person.

Homes

Disabled people are more likely than non-disabled people to live in a deprived area, and in poor housing.

There is a shortage of housing that is specifically designed to meet disabled people's needs.

84% of homes in England do not allow someone using a wheelchair to get to and through the front door easily and just **17%** of homes had level access or a wheelchair accessible toilet at entrance level.

Care and carers

For disabled adults a family member or relative normally provides assistance **(81%)**, followed by a friend or neighbour **(25%)**.

7 out of 10 families caring for someone with profound and multiple learning disabilities have reached or come close to 'breaking point' because of a lack of short break services.

Work

In 2015, the average hourly wage for disabled people was **£12.48**, compared to **£13.73** for non-disabled people.

Disabled people are nearly **4 times** as likely to be unemployed or involuntarily out of work as non-disabled people.

The high level of unemployment is the main reason why so many disabled people are in low income households.

Transport

Transport is the largest concern for disabled people in their local area. Pavement/road maintenance, access, and frequency of public transport are the biggest issues.

Disabled people travel **33% less often** than the general public.

60% of disabled people **do not have a car** available to their households, compared to **27%** of the overall population.

Crime

There are about **62,000** disability motivated hate crimes each year.

Disabled people are more likely to be victims of crime than non-disabled people.

40% of disability hate crimes involved violence against the person.

56% of disabled people said they had experienced hostility, aggression or violence from a stranger because of their condition or impairment.

Some issues

- If you imagine a journey you do every day, what would be the problems for someone with a disability?

- Could someone with a disability cope with your home, school or college?

- How could the financial problems of disabled people be eased?

- If you could make one change to improve the lives of disabled people, what would that be?

Source: Disability in the United Kingdom 2016,
www.papworthtrust.org.uk

Hearing loss

A hidden disability

 The term 'hearing loss' is used to cover all kinds of deafness.

There are **four** different **levels of hearing loss**, defined by the **quietest sound** that you are able to hear, measured in **decibels (dB)**.

Mild

Can't hear sound quieter than: **25-39dB**

This is about as loud as birdsong or the noise in a library. Can sometimes make following speech difficult, particularly in noisy situations or for long periods of time. People start avoiding social situations.

Moderate

Can't hear sound quieter than: **40-69dB**

This is about as loud as conversation in a restaurant, office or at home.. Often have difficulty following speech without hearing aids. Likely to avoid most or all social situations.

Severe

Can't hear sound quieter than: **70-94dB**

This is about as loud as a food blender or factory noise. Usually need to lipread or use sign language, even with hearing aids. May be eligible for cochlear implants.

Profound

Can't hear sound quieter than: **95dB**

This is about as loud as a motorbike or a power mower. Usually need to lipread or use sign language. Hearing aids often not helpful, may benefit from cochlear implants.

Across the UK
1 in 6 of us
(11 million people)
have hearing loss

Scotland
945,000

Northern Ireland
287,500

England
9,235,000

Wales
575,500

NB figures are estimates

There are **over 45,000** deaf children living in the UK and **20 million** deaf children in the world.

4 babies are born deaf every day.

Half of deaf children are born deaf and the other half become deaf during childhood.

Most hearing loss is age-related. **71.1%** of **over-70-year-olds** and **41.7%** of **over-50-year-olds** have some kind of hearing loss.

Noise-induced hearing loss is the next most common form of hearing loss. This occurs after prolonged exposure to excessive levels of noise. Sometimes, the effects of noise-induced hearing loss do not show until years later.

People working in industries with high levels of noise, such as **construction**, **the military, manufacturing** or **food processing** are the **most at risk** of developing noise-induced hearing loss.

Number of people with hearing loss in the UK, per age group

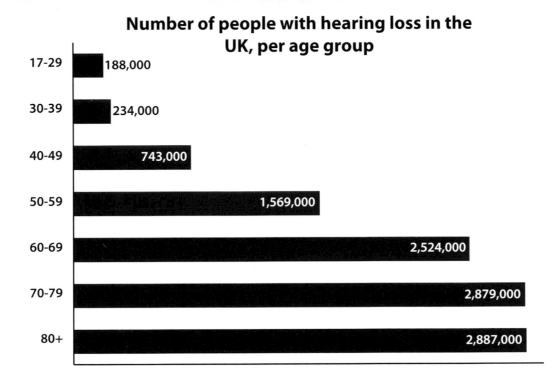

Age group	Number
17-29	188,000
30-39	234,000
40-49	743,000
50-59	1,569,000
60-69	2,524,000
70-79	2,879,000
80+	2,887,000

There are also an estimated 910,000 people in the UK who have severe or profound levels of deafness

Number of people with SEVERE/ PROFOUND hearing loss in the UK, per age group

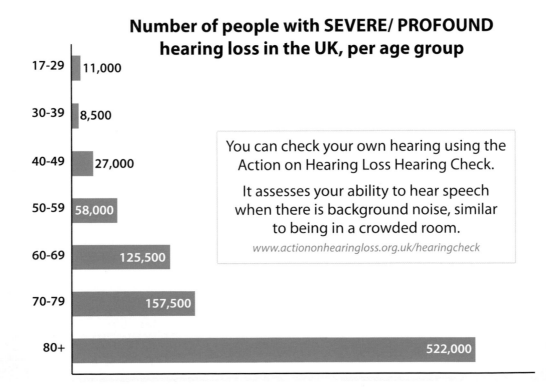

Age group	Number
17-29	11,000
30-39	8,500
40-49	27,000
50-59	58,000
60-69	125,500
70-79	157,500
80+	522,000

You can check your own hearing using the Action on Hearing Loss Hearing Check.

It assesses your ability to hear speech when there is background noise, similar to being in a crowded room.

www.actiononhearingloss.org.uk/hearingcheck

Risks of loud music

Approximately **5-10%** of people using personal music players such as smartphones listen at **high volumes** for **sustained periods of time**, putting themselves at risk of developing **noise-induced hearing** loss.

Noise exposure

People are often **not aware** of the dangers of noise exposure.

Repeated exposure to loud noise (eg from listening to music on smartphones too loudly) may cause **damage** to the **cochlea** and the **hearing nerve** and this can cause **permanent hearing loss** and **tinnitus**.

Excessive noise has been identified as the major, **avoidable** cause of hearing loss worldwide.

Tinnitus

Tinnitus is a **ringing** or **buzzing** sound in the ear or head that **isn't caused by an external noise**.

Around **one in every 10** UK adults has tinnitus and it is often due to prolonged exposure to **loud music**. The musicians **Plan B** and lead singer of **Coldplay, Chris Martin**, both suffer from tinnitus.

Tinnitus can have a **negative impact** on a person's **mental health, relationships** with family and friends and their ability to **sleep, concentrate** and **work**.

The number of people suffering from hearing loss in the UK is predicted to rise. By 2035 it is estimated that **15.6 million** (1 in 5) will suffer from hearing loss.

This is partly because the number of people exposed to high levels of noise at **nightclubs, live-music gigs**, or through a **personal music player** has **trebled** since the **1980s**.

Some issues

- What is the attraction of very loud music?

- How could young people be persuaded to protect their hearing?

- What might be the effect of a rise in the numbers of people with hearing loss?

- What sounds would you miss most if you could no longer hear them?

Source: Hearing Matters - Action on Hearing Loss
www.actiononhearingloss.org.uk

Sight loss

Around one person in 30 in the UK is living with sight loss

The Royal National Institute of Blind People (RNIB) estimates that around **2 million people in the UK** are living with sight loss. Around **360,000** of these people are **registered** as blind or partially sighted.

The most **common** impairments for people who are blind or partially sighted are: loss of **sharpness** or **clearness of vision**, loss of the **ability** to **detect objects** to either side or above or below the direction in which the person is looking , loss of **sensitivity** to contrast and loss of **colour vision.**

The UK population is **ageing** and as we get older we are **increasingly likely** to experience sight loss and there is an increase in some key **underlying causes** of sight loss, such as **obesity** and **diabetes**.

The RNIB predicts that by **2020** the number of people with sight loss in the UK will rise to over **2,250,000,** and by **2050,** the numbers will double to nearly **four million.**

Causes of sight loss

AMD - age related macular degeneration affects the central part of your retina, which is called the macula. It causes changes to your central vision which can make some everyday tasks like reading and driving difficult.

Cataract - cataracts occur when changes in the lens of the eye cause it to become less clear. This results in cloudy or misty vision.

Glaucoma - the optic nerve, which connects your eye to your brain, becomes damaged by the pressure of fluid inside the eye. It can lead to loss of vision if not detected and treated early on.

Refractive error - the shape of your eye does not bend light correctly, resulting in a blurred image.

Diabetic eye disease - a complication of diabetes, caused by high blood sugar levels damaging the back of the eye (retina). It can cause blindness if left undiagnosed and untreated.

This is the effect of macular degeneration on a person's sight.

Registering with a local authority can bring about **help** from **Social Services** and access to **benefits** and **concessions**.

You have to have **permanent** changes in vision in **both eyes** which **can't be corrected** by wearing **glasses** in order to be registered with your local authority as **sight impaired** (partially sighted) or **severely sight impaired** (blind).

Someone who had lost the sight in **one eye**, for example, **could not register** unless the sight in their **other** eye was also **damaged**.

Number of people on the registers of blind or partially sighted people
(England only, 2014, latest available data)

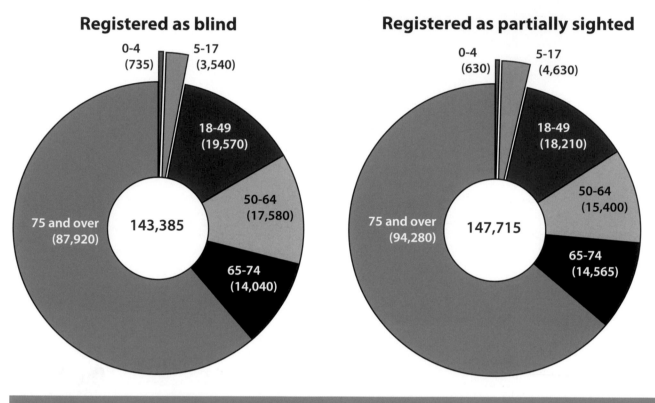

Registered as blind

- 0-4 (735)
- 5-17 (3,540)
- 18-49 (19,570)
- 50-64 (17,580)
- 65-74 (14,040)
- 75 and over (87,920)

143,385

Registered as partially sighted

- 0-4 (630)
- 5-17 (4,630)
- 18-49 (18,210)
- 50-64 (15,400)
- 65-74 (14,565)
- 75 and over (94,280)

147,715

| Symbol | Guide | Long | Banded |

The white cane is one of the symbols most closely associated with sight loss - but people are often not aware of the different functions of canes: as a symbol - just to make other people aware, as a guide to find obstacles, a long cane helps people with little or no vision to find obstacles, a red and white banded cane shows that the person has a hearing loss as well as sight loss.

Things Not To Say To A Blind Person

"You don't look blind."

"I get it a lot in the Paralympics as well. They say, "Well you don't look like you're blind so I bet you're lying. I bet you're just doing that so that you can run with like, slower people. I'm like, "Well you don't look stupid but I'm pretty sure you are."

From the BBC Three Programme: Things Not To Say To A Blind Person

Sight loss in children and young people

2 in every 1,000 children and young people up to the age of 25 in the UK have vision impairment. The true figure is probably higher as it does not include children who have difficulty seeing but don't match the specific definition.

5 in every 10,000 of children up to the age of 16 are severely sight impaired/blind.

An estimated **31 in every 100,000** children and young people under 19 in the UK have both vision and hearing impairments.

Children and young people from certain groups are at a higher risk of vision impairment:

- very **premature** and very **low birth weight** babies;
- those with **learning difficulties**;
- those from the most **economically deprived** backgrounds.

Around **20%** of young people with vision impairment have **additional special educational needs** and /or **disabilities** and a further **30%** have **complex needs**.

Two thirds of childhood vision impairment was present from **birth** or diagnosed in the **first year of life**.

About **7 in 10** children and young people with vision impairment attend **mainstream** schools.

Around **1 in 3** go to **special** schools dealing with a variety of disabilities.

Very few are in schools specifically for pupils with vision impairment.

Young people with vision impairment are twice as likely - **44%** - as their sighted peers **not** to be in **employment**, **education** or **training**.

Some issues

- What would worry you most if you found you were losing your sight?

- Which is better, to be in the same school as everyone else or to be in a school with special facilities?

- What do we do to make life easier for people with sight loss? What more could be done?

- What is your most recent experience involving a person with vision impairment?

Source: The Royal National Institute of Blind People, rnib.org.uk

Environment

Weather disasters

The human cost of disasters 1995-2015

Between 1995 and 2015, 90% of disasters have been caused by floods, storms, heatwaves and other weather-related events.

In total, **6,457** weather-related disasters were recorded worldwide by the Centre for Research on the Epidemiology of Disasters (CRED) which updates the Emergency Events Database EM-DAT.

Over this period, weather-related disasters claimed **606,000 lives**, an average of **30,000 per year**, with an **additional 4.1 billion** people injured, left homeless or in need of emergency assistance.

On average, **205 million people** were affected by such disasters each year.

Weather-related disasters became increasingly frequent in the late 1990s, peaking at **401** events in 2005.

A sustained rise in the number of floods and storms pushed the average annual total up to **335** disasters per year after 2005, **14%** higher than in the previous decade and more than twice the level recorded in 1980-1989.

Occurrences of natural disasters by disaster type

(EM-DAT classifies disasters according to the type of hazard that provokes them. This information is based on hydrological, meteorological and climatological disasters which collectively make up weather-related disasters)

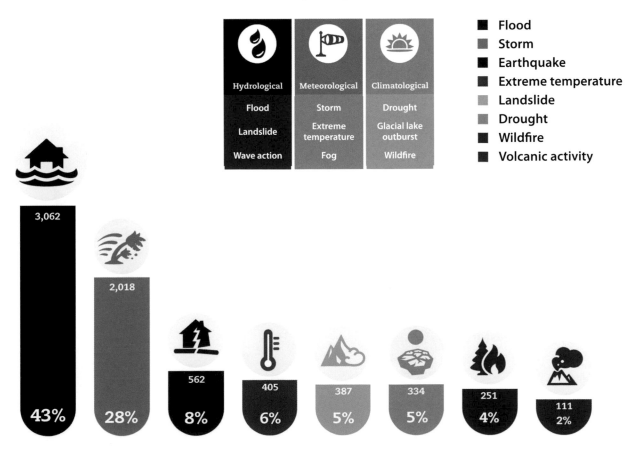

Hydrological	Meteorological	Climatological
Flood	Storm	Drought
Landslide	Extreme temperature	Glacial lake outburst
Wave action	Fog	Wildfire

- ■ Flood
- ■ Storm
- ■ Earthquake
- ■ Extreme temperature
- ■ Landslide
- ■ Drought
- ■ Wildfire
- ■ Volcanic activity

3,062 — 43%
2,018 — 28%
562 — 8%
405 — 6%
387 — 5%
334 — 5%
251 — 4%
111 — 2%

Figures do not add up to 100% due to rounding

Asia was hit hardest

Asia had more frequent weather-related disasters and greater numbers of people killed and affected than any other continent. This is due mainly to Asia's large and varied landmass, including multiple river basins, flood plains and other zones at high risk from natural hazards, plus high population densities in disaster-prone regions.

In total, **2,495** weather-related disasters struck Asia between 1995 and 2015, **affecting 3.7 billion** people and **killing** a further **332,000** individuals.

USA and China reported the highest numbers of weather-related disasters during this period.

Myanmar: A girl rides her bicycle through an area affected by flooding

The 2008 Cyclone Nargis caused at least 138,000 deaths in Myanmar

Number of weather-related disasters reported per country

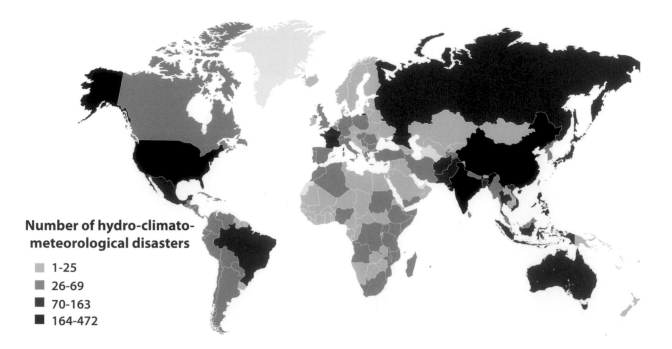

Number of hydro-climato-meteorological disasters

- 1-25
- 26-69
- 70-163
- 164-472

Number of people AFFECTED by weather-related disasters
(NB DEATHS are EXCLUDED from the total affected)

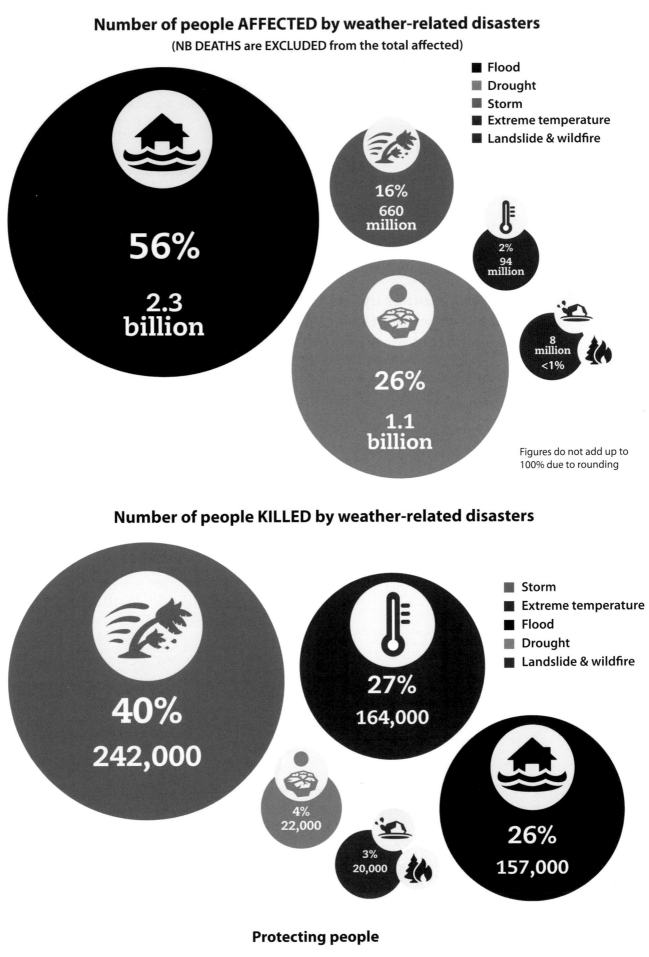

Legend:
- Flood
- Drought
- Storm
- Extreme temperature
- Landslide & wildfire

56% 2.3 billion

16% 660 million

2% 94 million

8 million <1%

26% 1.1 billion

Figures do not add up to 100% due to rounding

Number of people KILLED by weather-related disasters

Legend:
- Storm
- Extreme temperature
- Flood
- Drought
- Landslide & wildfire

40% 242,000

27% 164,000

4% 22,000

3% 20,000

26% 157,000

Protecting people

More effective use of storm early warning systems could save many more lives in future, particularly in poor rural communities at higher risk.
Proven life-saving measures, such as cyclone shelters and wind-resistant buildings, are also options which may help protect vulnerable populations.

Greatest effect on human life

China and **India**, dominate the league table of countries **most affected** by weather-related disasters because both have large populations.

Together these two nations account for more than **3 billion** disaster-affected people between 1995 and 2015 - **75%** of the global total of **4.1 billion people.**

Brazil is the only country from the Americas appearing in the top 10 list, and **Kenya** and **Ethiopia** are the only African nations.

When we look at the rate - the number of people affected per 100,000 inhabitants - the global picture looks very different. **Six** of the **most affected** countries are now in **Africa**, and just **three** in **Asia**.

Moldova is the only European country appearing on either list. It is sixth in the rate table, due mainly to a storm in 2000 that affected **2.6 million** people out of a total population of **3.6 million.**

Top ten countries by TOTAL POPULATION AFFECTED by weather-related disasters compared with the top ten countries most affected PER 100,000 INHABITANTS

■ Countries with the highest proportion of affected people over the total population (per 100,000 inhabitants)

■ Countries with the highest absolute number of affected people (in millions)

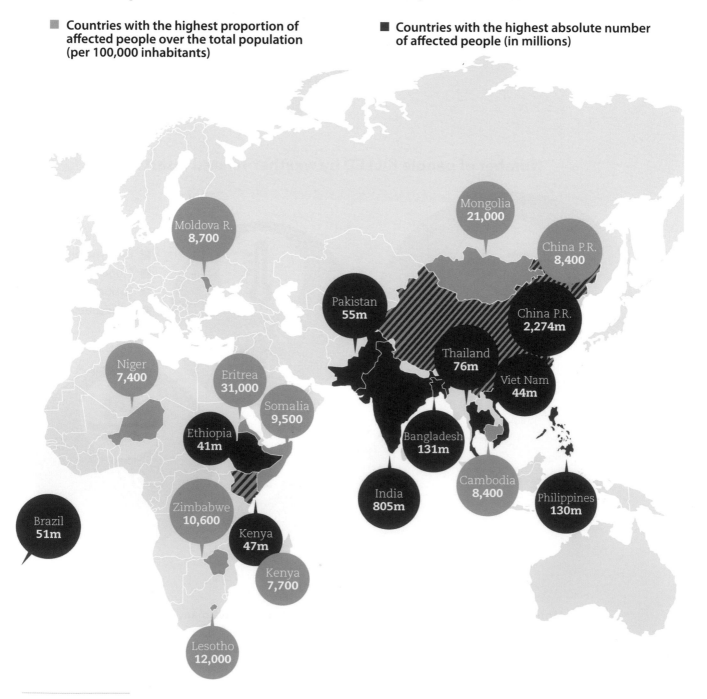

When countries are grouped together by income, the highest numbers of weather-related disasters occurred in lower-middle-income countries.

■ High-income countries
eg Argentina, Japan, UK

■ Upper-middle-income countries
eg China, Mongolia, Paraguay

■ Lower middle-income countries
eg Bangladesh, Myanmar, Ukraine

■ Low income countries
eg Afghanistan, Nepal, Somalia

Number of deaths and percentage of weather-related disasters, per income group

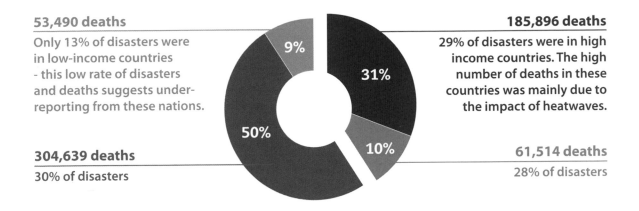

53,490 deaths

Only 13% of disasters were in low-income countries - this low rate of disasters and deaths suggests under-reporting from these nations.

185,896 deaths

29% of disasters were in high income countries. The high number of deaths in these countries was mainly due to the impact of heatwaves.

304,639 deaths

30% of disasters

61,514 deaths

28% of disasters

Loss of homes and facilities

87 million homes were damaged or destroyed by weather-related disasters since 1995, plus **130,000** damaged or destroyed schools, clinics, hospitals and other critical health and education facilities.

Floods and storms together accounted for around **98%** of houses damaged and **99.9%** of education health and education facilities.

Often, one single event had a devastating impact: Cyclone Sidr destroyed more than **4,000** schools in **Bangladesh** in 2007; **Peru** lost **600** health facilities in one cyclone in 1997, while a tropical cyclone in 1999 devastated **11,000** schools in **India**.

In April 2015, a flood in **Peru** damaged **614** schools and more than **17,000** houses.

In 2015, **Bangladesh** was hit by two storms in April and June that respectively destroyed **29,000** and **33,000** homes.

> **Population growth will continue to put more and more people in harm's way, while uncontrolled building on flood plains and storm-prone coastal zones will increase human vulnerabilities to extreme weather events.**

Some issues

- Are there any reasons for the increase in weather-related disasters?

- Why aren't more measures taken to prevent the damage to homes and facilities in poor countries?

- What can the rest of the world do to help the poorest countries?

- The UK also seems to have suffered from more flooding than previously. What could be done about this?

Source: The Human Cost of Weather Related Disasters 1995-2015
www.emdat.be

Air pollution...

...the invisible killer

Particulate matter (PM) in the air affects more people than any other pollutant.

It is a mixture of solid particles and liquid droplets. Some particles, such as dust, dirt, soot, or smoke, are large or dark enough to be seen with the naked eye. Others are so small they can only be detected using an electron microscope. Tiny particles pose the greatest problems, because they can get deep into your lungs, and some may even get into your bloodstream.

Exposure to ozone (O3), nitrogen dioxide (NO2) and sulphur dioxide (SO2) also pose serious risks to health.

Ozone at ground level (which is not the same as the ozone layer in the upper atmosphere) is one of the main causes of smog. Excessive O3 can cause breathing problems, trigger asthma, reduce lung function and cause lung diseases.

NO2 from processes like heating, power generation, and engines in vehicles and ships, and SO2 from the burning of fossil fuels (eg coal and oil) for domestic heating, power generation and motor vehicles can play a role in asthma, bronchial symptoms, lung inflammation and reduced lung function.

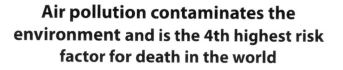

Air pollution contaminates the environment and is the 4th highest risk factor for death in the world

In September 2016, the World Health Organization (WHO) estimated that the diseases caused by exposure to outdoor and indoor (household) pollution were responsible for **more than 6 million deaths – 1 in 9** of total deaths globally.

Number of deaths caused by exposure to air pollution

Outdoor air pollution
Caused by emissions from things like: power generation, transportation, agriculture, open burning, household pollution

Household air pollution
Caused by burning solid fuels for heating and cooking, including: coal, wood, dung

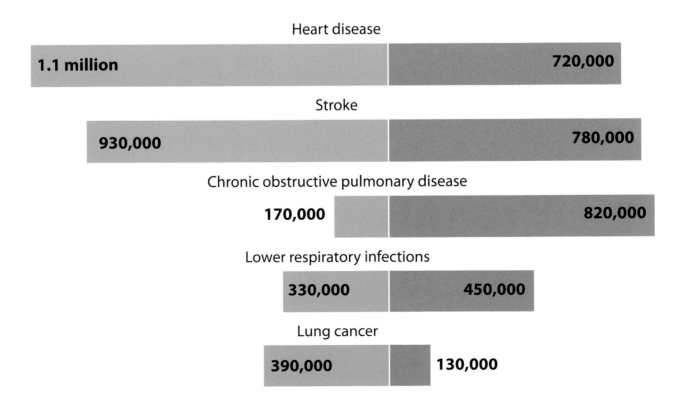

Heart disease

1.1 million **720,000**

Stroke

930,000 **780,000**

Chronic obstructive pulmonary disease

170,000 **820,000**

Lower respiratory infections

330,000 **450,000**

Lung cancer

390,000 **130,000**

3 million deaths a year are linked to exposure to OUTDOOR air pollution

Nearly **90%** of air-pollution-related deaths occur in low- and middle-income countries - nearly **2 out of 3** are in the South-East Asia and Western Pacific regions.

In China and India, **less than 1%** of the population lives in areas which meet WHO air quality guidelines

The '*WHO air quality guidelines*' assess the impact pollution has on health, and shows where pollution levels are most harmful to health.

In 2016, **92%** of the world population was living in places where these guidelines levels were not met.

Deaths from air pollution worldwide

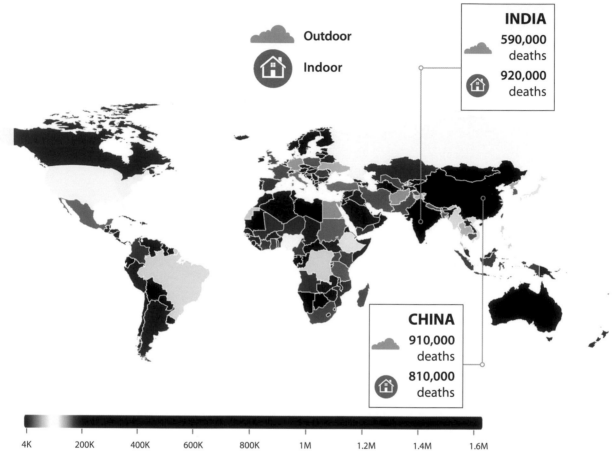

Outdoor

Indoor

INDIA
590,000 deaths
920,000 deaths

CHINA
910,000 deaths
810,000 deaths

4K 200K 400K 600K 800K 1M 1.2M 1.4M 1.6M

"*Air pollution continues take a toll on the health of the most vulnerable populations – women, children and older adults...*

For people to be healthy, they must breathe clean air from their first breath to their last."

Dr Bustreo
Assistant Director-General, WHO

Some issues

- Is there anything you could do now, or in the near future, about air pollution?

- What can and should governments do?

- Where would you start to combat pollution - would you restrict traffic, industry, power generation? Or something else?

Source: Global Burden of Disease Study, The Lancet; World Health Organization (WHO)
www.thelancet.com
http://www.who.int/en

Light pollution

Britain's darkest and most light-polluted skies

What is light pollution?

Light pollution refers to artificial light which shines where it is neither wanted nor needed.

There are three types of light pollution:

skyglow – the pink or orange glow we see for miles around towns and cities, spreading deep into the countryside, caused by a scattering of artificial light by airborne dust and water droplets;

glare – the uncomfortable brightness of a light source;

light intrusion – light spilling beyond the boundary of the property on which a light is located, sometimes shining through windows and curtains.

If there is light pollution in an area, then people cannot see the night sky and stars properly.

Impact on wildlife...

Light pollution interrupts natural rhythms including migration, reproduction and feeding patterns. Man-made light can confuse migrating birds, often with fatal outcomes. You can often hear birds singing late at night in trees lit by a streetlight.

...and humans

A survey from the Campaign to Protect Rural England (CPRE) found that light pollution can cause a great deal of distress to humans too, including disrupted sleep.

Recent studies suggest that exposure to light at night can interfere with the production of melatonin, a brain hormone which has a role in resetting the body's biological clock.

Bath city skyglow

Satellite images taken at 1.30am during September 2015 give an accurate picture of how much light is spilling into the night sky over Britain.

Heavily lit areas such as major roads, ports and airports, show up clearly on the map.

It also shows that there are many areas with very little light pollution, where people could expect to see a truly dark night sky.

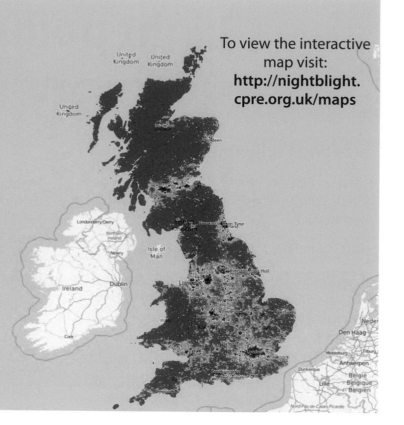

To view the interactive map visit: http://nightblight. cpre.org.uk/maps

To compare different light levels over Britain, the data from the satellite images was split into nine colour categories - ranging from **dark blues** (darkest) to **dark reds** (brightest)

This showed that **only 22%** of England had night skies completely free of light pollution.

Combining the two **darkest** categories means that **49%** of **England** can be considered dark, compared with **almost 75%** of **Wales** and **87.5%** of **Scotland**.

There are higher levels of light pollution in England in all the categories.

Comparison of light pollution levels

Colour band	England	Wales	Scotland
1 (darkest skies)	21.7%	56.9%	76.8%
2	27.3%	18.0%	10.7%
3	19.1%	9.3%	4.6%
4	11.0%	5.8%	2.8%
5	6.8%	3.8%	1.7%
6	5.0%	2.9%	1.2%
7	4.3%	2.1%	1.0%
8	3.2%	1.0%	0.9%
9 (brightest skies)	1.6%	0.2%	0.3%

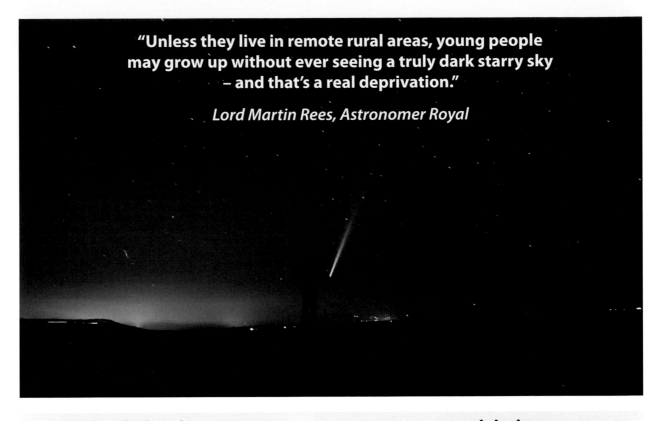

> "Unless they live in remote rural areas, young people may grow up without ever seeing a truly dark starry sky – and that's a real deprivation."
>
> *Lord Martin Rees, Astronomer Royal*

England's brightest areas...

The highest levels of light pollution were around towns and cities, such as London, Leeds, Manchester, Liverpool, Birmingham and Newcastle.

19 of the brightest 20 skies are above **London** boroughs.

Manchester is the only non-London district in the top 20.

...and darkest

The Isles of Scilly, **West Devon** and **Eden in Cumbria** were the darkest areas in England.

The very darkest spot in England was a hillside on the East Kielder Moors in Northumberland.

53% of our darkest skies are over National Parks and Areas of Outstanding Natural Beauty.

Street lights

One of the main sources of light pollution is street lighting.

The **top five** counties with the highest amount of unspoilt dark skies - Herefordshire, Northumberland, Cumbria, Devon and North Yorkshire - are making changes to their street lighting.

The future

Advances in lighting technology mean that upward light pollution can be minimised without compromising road safety or increasing crime.

Some issues

- Have you ever been somewhere where you can really see the night sky?

- Lord Rees says young people are being deprived of seeing a dark sky. Does that feel like a deprivation to you?

- How might we help our bodies to avoid the biological issues connected to light pollution?

- Some councils have suggested turning off street lighting very late at night to early morning. Would you support this idea?

Source: Night Blight: Mapping England's light pollution and dark skies - Campaign to Protect Rural England (CPRE) http://www.cpre.org.uk

Fly-tipping

The illegal dumping of waste is anti-social behaviour which affects our environment

What is fly-tipping?

Fly-tipping refers to household, industrial, or commercial waste that is dumped illegally. It often includes items such as garden refuse and larger domestic items such as fridges or mattresses. It can be a source of pollution; a potential danger to public health and a hazard to wildlife.

Licensed companies charge for taking away people's waste, then deposit it at waste disposal sites where they are charged to do so but some **unlicensed** companies might charge less, then dump it illegally in fields, lay-bys or at roadsides so they don't incur the waste disposal site charge.

Some other reasons behind fly-tipping might be:

- a lack of waste disposal facilities nearby;

- an assumption that someone else will clear up the waste.

Who is responsible?

- **Local authorities** are responsible for investigating and clearing small scale fly-tipping on public land (including public roads and highways within their responsibility).

- **The Environment Agency** investigates larger scale fly-tipping (more than a lorry load of waste), hazardous waste and fly-tipping by organised gangs, but these incidents are not included in these figures.

- **Private landowners** are responsible for the clearance of fly-tipped waste on their private land and incidents are not included in these figures.

Fly tipping 2014/15, England

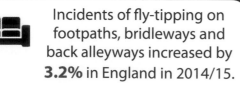 Local authorities dealt with **900,000** incidents of fly-tipping - an increase of **5.6%** since 2013/14.

Incidents of fly-tipping on footpaths, bridleways and back alleyways increased by **3.2%** in England in 2014/15.

Together these now make up **28%** of fly-tipping incidents.

 There were **436,000** fly-tipping incidents on highways, making up **48%** of total incidents.

Small, van-load size, fly-tipping incidents accounted for **31%** of total incidents and **30%** were tipping from a car boot.

 There were **590,000** household waste incidents, which made up **66%** of total incidents.

£ The cost of fly-tipping

Local authorities spent
£17.6 million on nearly
515,000 enforcement actions.

The actions included:
315,000 investigations,

75,000 warning letters,

38,000 statutory notices served
on owners and occupiers to clean
up privately-owned land and
property where fly-tipping has
occurred,

45,000 duty of care inspections
ensuring people were handling
their waste correctly, and

42,000 other enforcement actions.

There were an **151 additional
incidents** of large scale illegal
dumping dealt with by the
Environment Agency

The cost of fly-tipping on private
land is estimated to be between
£50 - £150 million a year.

Fines and punishment

Fly-tipping is a criminal offence which can result in a fine of **up to £50,000** or **12 months imprisonment** if there is a conviction in a Magistrates' Court.

An **unlimited fine** and **up to 5 years imprisonment** can be given if there is a conviction in a Crown Court.

There can also be **fixed penalty notices** - which are 'on the spot' fines of between **£150-£400**. You can either pay the penalty within the timescale shown on the notice, or you may be prosecuted in court.

A vehicle can be seized and/or its contents if it is suspected that it has been involved in fly tipping.

Local authorities carried out **1,810** prosecutions for fly-tipping offences in 2014/15 - over **98%** resulted in a **conviction**, **82%** resulted in a **fine** and there were **21** cases of imprisonment.

Some issues

- What is the worst incident of fly-tipping you have seen?

- What would you like to say to people who fly-tip?

- What else could be done to prevent this happening?

Source: Department for Environment, Food and Rural Affairs
© Crown copyright 2015
www.gov.uk/government/organisations/
department-for-environment-food-rural-affairs
House of Commons Library - Fly-tipping - the illegal dumping of waste
www.parliament.uk

Family & relationships

Trends in baby names

The most popular names for...

...boys

	2005	2010	2015
1	Jack	Oliver	Oliver
2	Joshua	Jack	Jack
3	Thomas	Harry	Harry
4	James	Alfie	George
5	Oliver	Charlie	Jacob
6	Daniel	Thomas	Charlie
7	Samuel	William	Noah
8	William	Joshua	William
9	Harry	George	Thomas
10	Joseph	James	Oscar

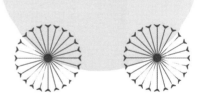

... and girls

	2005	2010	2015
1	Jessica	Olivia	Amelia
2	Emily	Sophie	Olivia
3	Sophie	Emily	Emily
4	Olivia	Lily	Isla
5	Ellie	Amelia	Ava
6	Chloe	Jessica	Ella
7	Grace	Ruby	Jessica
8	Lucy	Chloe	Isabella
9	Charlotte	Grace	Mia
10	Ella	Evie	Poppy

Amelia ranked 15th in 2005

How many babies?

In 2015:

There were **697,852** live births in England and Wales.

The babies were given **over 27,000** different **boys'** names and **over 35,000** different **girls'** names.

6,941 babies were given the name **Oliver** and **5,158** were called **Amelia**.

New entries to the top 100 most popular baby names for boys and girls, England & Wales

There were 4 new names for boys:
Jaxon, Roman, Reggie and Carter; and

6 new names for girls:
Penelope, Mila, Clara, Arabella, Maddison and Aria.

Regional differences

In Wales and in 7 out of the 9 English regions Amelia was the most popular girls' name and Oliver the most popular boys' name.

In 2 regions, West Midlands and London, Muhammad was the most popular boys' name.

In the East Midlands and the East of England the most popular girls' name was Olivia.

Spelling matters

It has sometimes been reported that **Muhammad** is the most popular name for baby boys in the UK – however this is often because people have combined the various spellings of this name.

The statistics are based on the exact spelling of the name given on the birth certificate. Grouping names with similar pronunciation but different spellings would mean making subjective decisions and would change the rankings: eg are Sophie, Sophia and Sofia the same name?

If they were all combined they would knock Amelia off the top spot on the 2015 girls' list.

Most popular baby names in Scotland

1	Jack	1	Emily
2	Oliver	2	Sophie
3	James	3	Olivia
4	Lewis	4	Isla
5	Alexander	5	Ava
6	Charlie	6	Jessica
7	Logan	7	Amelia
8	Lucas	8	Ella
9	Harris	9	Lucy
10=	Daniel, Finlay, Jacob	10	Lily

There were 55,098 live births in Scotland in 2015

Most popular baby names in Northern Ireland

1	James	1	Emily
2	Jack	2	Ella
3	Noah	3	Grace
4	Charlie	4	Sophie
5	Daniel	5	Olivia
6	Oliver	6	Anna
7	Matthew	7	Amelia
8	Harry	8	Aoife
9	Thomas	9	Lucy
10	Jake	10	Ava

Final figures are not available but projected NI births for 2015 were 1,851 so numbers for each name are likely to be low.

A survey of 1,581 adults asked how they felt about their own names and about naming children

How do you feel about your own first name?

68% of those asked liked their name and

67% thought their name suited them.

Who is it acceptable to name a child after?

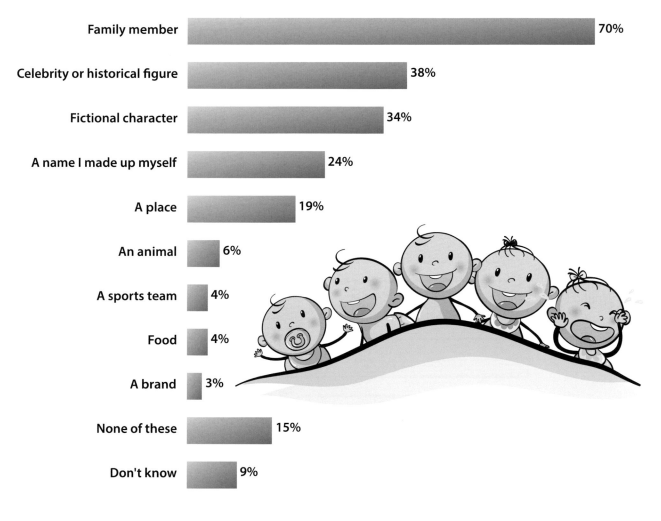

- Family member — 70%
- Celebrity or historical figure — 38%
- Fictional character — 34%
- A name I made up myself — 24%
- A place — 19%
- An animal — 6%
- A sports team — 4%
- Food — 4%
- A brand — 3%
- None of these — 15%
- Don't know — 9%

Would you give your child the same first name as you?

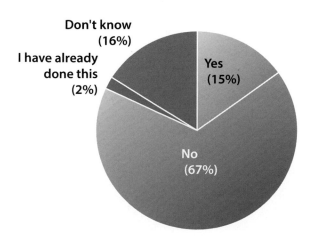

- Don't know (16%)
- I have already done this (2%)
- Yes (15%)
- No (67%)

Some issues

- Do you feel that a name should be traditional or original?

- Why do names matter?

- Are there some names which affect your chances in life?

Sources: Baby names in England and Wales: 2015, ONS, www.ons.gov.uk
Population Projections for Northern Ireland, www.nisra.gov.uk
Births by sex, Scotland, www.nrscotland.gov.uk

Childcare

UK families spend a third of their income on childcare. But not all families can afford it

Parents in Britain spend almost a third of their incomes on childcare – more than anywhere else in the world - and such high costs have the greatest consequences for the poorest families. Of those families in severe poverty, nearly half have cut back on food to afford childcare and **58%** said they were or would be no better off working once childcare is paid for.

Net percentage of family income spent on childcare costs, within OECD selected countries

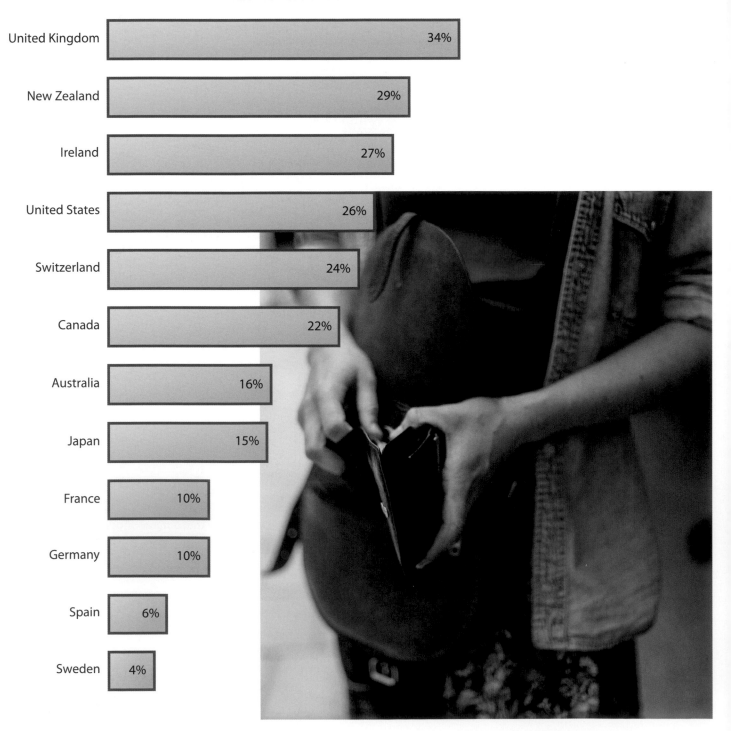

Country	%
United Kingdom	34%
New Zealand	29%
Ireland	27%
United States	26%
Switzerland	24%
Canada	22%
Australia	16%
Japan	15%
France	10%
Germany	10%
Spain	6%
Sweden	4%

Poverty

The cost of childcare is pushing the poorest out of work and pushing more children into poverty. Because childcare is so expensive, families on low-incomes across the UK are having to turn down jobs. They are even considering leaving work because they can't afford to pay for childcare, according to new research from Save the Children and the Daycare Trust.

But having at least one parent in work significantly reduces the risk of severe child poverty - which is defined as having a household income of less than **£12,000** per year.

Only **6%** of children in these families. are in severe poverty compared to **43%** of children in workless household

A quarter of parents in severe poverty have given up work and a third have turned down a job mainly because of high childcare costs – more than twice as many as better off parents.

Of those parents who live in severe poverty and are currently in paid employment the majority **(80%)** agreed with the statement "Once I have paid for childcare, I am in a similar position to as if I was not working".

The majority of parents living in severe poverty (61%) said they were struggling to pay for childcare. This compares to around a third of parents on higher incomes **(37%).**

Families in severe poverty were twice as likely as better off families to move home because of the high costs of childcare. **26%** of parents in severe poverty have been unable to take up education or training because of high childcare costs.

Whatever their level of income, **63%** of parents, say they can't afford not to work but **struggle** to pay for childcare.

A quarter of parents said the cost of childcare has caused them to get into **debt**.

The costs of childcare are on a level with mortgage or rent payments for **41%** of families.

Sally Copley, Save the Children's Head of Poverty, said: "The government is undermining its own 'make work pay' policy by not funding the costs of childcare for the poorest families."

Some issues

- Why do you think childcare is so expensive?

- If poorer families cannot afford childcare, how will they earn money to survive?

- Why do you think the government does not provide childcare for those in need?

- How can we make sure parents get the support they need to be able to work?

- What could explain the difference in costs between countries?

Source: OECD and Save The Children
www.oecd.org/unitedkingdom
www.savethechildren.org.uk

Living with parents

**More young adults are living with their parents -
and it is men who are most likely to stay at home**

Men and women, aged 20-34, living with parents, UK, 2016

2.0 million	1.3 million
31% of all men aged 20-34	20% of all women aged 20-34

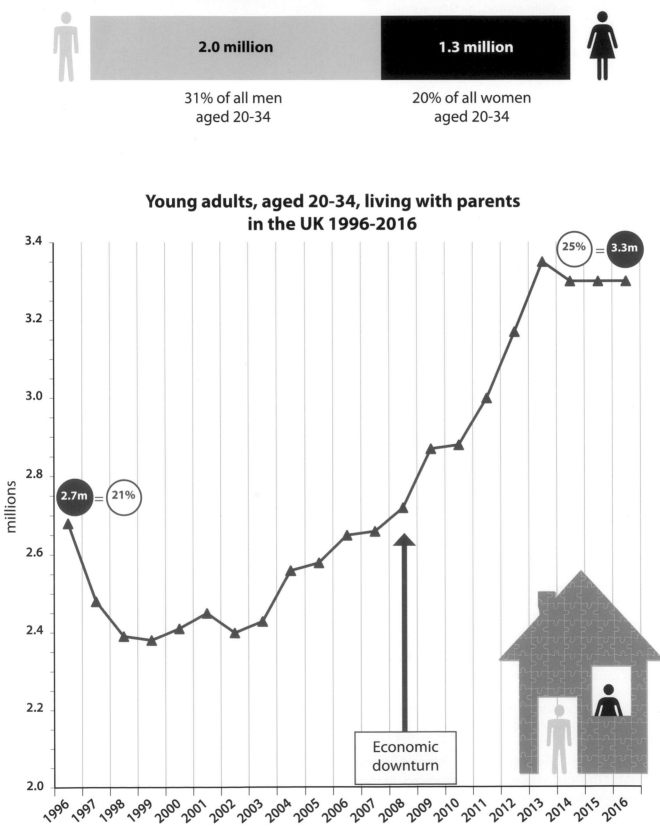

Young adults, aged 20-34, living with parents in the UK 1996-2016

millions

25% = 3.3m

2.7m = 21%

Economic downturn

1996 1997 1998 1999 2000 2001 2002 2003 2004 2005 2006 2007 2008 2009 2010 2011 2012 2013 2014 2015 2016

Percentage of men and women aged 20-34 living with parents by age, UK, 2016

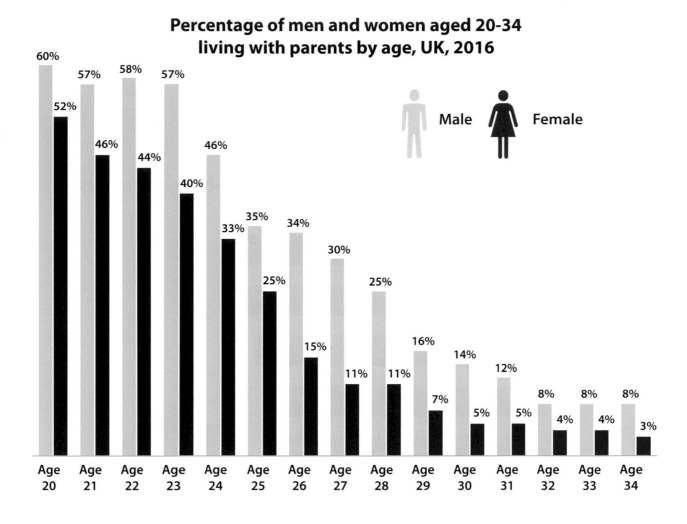

Male   Female

	Male	Female
Age 20	60%	52%
Age 21	57%	46%
Age 22	58%	44%
Age 23	57%	40%
Age 24	46%	33%
Age 25	35%	25%
Age 26	34%	15%
Age 27	30%	11%
Age 28	25%	11%
Age 29	16%	7%
Age 30	14%	5%
Age 31	12%	5%
Age 32	8%	4%
Age 33	8%	4%
Age 34	8%	3%

Large numbers of young adults are tending to stay at home for longer.

Reasons for this might be because:

- they are staying in education and training for longer;

- they are forming relationships (ie getting married, forming a civil partnership or cohabiting with a partner) at older ages;

- it has become more expensive to rent or buy a home. Saving for a deposit is seen as one of the biggest hurdles to home ownership;

- young women are more likely to become lone parents when a relationship breaks down and move back to live with their parents;

- if you're single and under 35, you can only get Housing Benefit for bed-sit accommodation or a single room in shared accommodation - this may encourage young males to move back to their parents after the breakdown of a relationship.

Country comparisons

In some countries around the world a high proportion of young people still live at home with their parents.

This trend is most noticeable in countries which were badly affected by the global financial crisis.

Percentage of young people aged 15-29 living with their parents

(selected OECD countries, 2014)

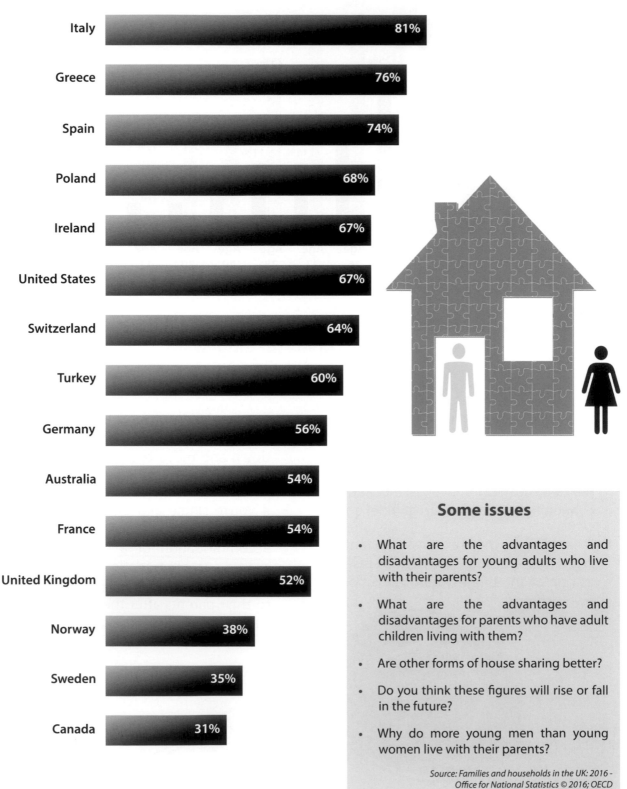

Country	Percentage
Italy	81%
Greece	76%
Spain	74%
Poland	68%
Ireland	67%
United States	67%
Switzerland	64%
Turkey	60%
Germany	56%
Australia	54%
France	54%
United Kingdom	52%
Norway	38%
Sweden	35%
Canada	31%

Some issues

- What are the advantages and disadvantages for young adults who live with their parents?

- What are the advantages and disadvantages for parents who have adult children living with them?

- Are other forms of house sharing better?

- Do you think these figures will rise or fall in the future?

- Why do more young men than young women live with their parents?

Source: Families and households in the UK: 2016 - Office for National Statistics © 2016; OECD
www.ons.gov.uk www.oecd.org

Bullying

More than half of young people have sometimes used bullying behaviour

What is bullying?

People can have a different idea of the behaviours that are considered to be bullying.

But there are some behaviours that everyone recognises as bullying.

For their annual Bullying Survey, Ditch the Label, an anti-bullying charity, interviewed 8,850 young people aged 12-20 and asked all of them, regardless of their experience of bullying, if they had ever done any of the things listed below.

58% had done at least one.

Have you ever said something to **purposely upset** someone?

33% have

37% of males have, 27% of females have and 47% of transgender have done this.

Have you ever **physically attacked** somebody?

20% have

29% of males have, 11% of females have and 43% of trans have.

Have you purposely **excluded somebody** from a social group?

19% have

20% of males have, 17% of females have and 42% of trans have.

Have you ever **said something nasty** to somebody online?

27% have

31% of males have, 23% of females have and 42% of trans have.

Have you ever **taken or damaged somebody's things** to upset them?

9% have

12% of males have, 4% of females have and 32% of trans have.

Have you ever **started a rumour** about somebody?

NB only 1% of those surveyed identified as transgender

13% have

16% of males have, 10% of females have and 33% of trans have.

Neither bully nor victim

Ditch the Label, who conducted the survey, never call anybody a 'bully' or a 'victim', because they don't see bullying as an identity. Just because somebody experiences bullying, it doesn't make them a victim.

Bullying is a behaviour and like all behaviours, there is a root cause and a remedy for change.

To help bring about that change they devoted part of their survey to examining two sub-groups: the people who said they had **ever bullied someone** and the people who said they had **bullied someone on a daily basis** - as well as people who **had been bullied.**

Why do people bully?

Who is responsible?   What different groups think

"The person doing the bullying is JEALOUS of something"

- 70% on average agree
  - 65% who have bullied agree
  - 48% who have bullied daily agree

  - 72% who have been bullied agree
  - 68% who have been bullied daily agree

"The person being bullied needs to CHANGE "

- 10% on average agree
  - 18% who have bullied agree
  - 31% who have bullied daily agree

  - 13% who have been bullied agree
  - 18% who have been bullied daily agree

"The person doing the bullying was going through a TOUGH TIME "

- 43% on average agree
  - 46% who have bullied agree
  - 41% who have bullied daily agree

  - 43% who have been bullied agree
  - 37% who have been bullied daily agree

"People get bullied because they did something to DESERVE it"

- 19% on average agree
  - 32% who have bullied agree
  - 48% who have bullied daily agree

  - 17% who have been bullied agree
  - 19% who have been bullied daily agree

"The person doing the bullying should CHANGE"

- 38% on average agree
  - 40% who have bullied agree
  - 36% who have bullied daily agree

  - 39% who have been bullied agree
  - 40% who have been bullied daily agree

"People get bullied because they are DIFFERENT IN SOME WAY "

- 71% on average agree
  - 74% who have bullied agree
  - 64% who have bullied daily agree

  - 77% who have been bullied agree
  - 73% who have been bullied daily agree

Those who were bullied in the past year... were asked How frequently were you bullied?

Daily	Several times a week	Once a week	Once a fortnight	Once a month	Once a term	Once every six months	Once a year
11%	19%	16%	9%	12%	11%	12%	10%

Why do you think you were bullied?

- **52%** Attitudes towards my appearance
- **43%** Attitudes towards interest/hobby
- **21%** Attitudes towards my high grades
- **19%** Attitudes towards my family's income
- **19%** Because a family member or friend was also bullied
- **17%** Attitudes towards my low grades
- **17%** Attitudes towards my perceived masculinity/femininity
- **16%** Attitudes towards a family issue made public
- **10%** Attitudes towards a disability I have
- **8%** Racist bullying or comments
- **7%** Attitudes towards my sexuality
- **7%** Attitudes towards my religion
- **6%** Attitudes towards my cultural identity
- **5%** Attitudes towards my gender identity or expression

What to do

The survey suggests that **145,800** young people were **bullied today and every day.**

Bullying should never be ignored.
If you are bullying or being bullied seek help:

Bullying UK:
bullying.co.uk or call 0808 800 2222

Ditch the Label:
ditchthelabel.org

Childline:
childline.org.uk or call 08001111

Some issues

- Do any of these results surprise you?

- Why do you think people bully?

- Do bullies deserve help?

- How can bullies be helped?

- What can you do to make sure people can seek help if they are bullied?

Source: Annual Bullying Survey 2016 www.ditchthelabel.org

Finance

Debt snapshot

The number of people seeking help with debt problems hit a record high in 2016

How many people are in debt and how much do they owe?

313,679 people contacted the StepChange Debt Charity for advice in the first half of 2016.

They owed an average of **£13,826** each - with each person having on average **5.7 different debts**.

This did **not** include amounts people owed for things like essential household bills or loans from family and friends, which were still outstanding after the date payment was due. These debts are known as **arrears**.

Who is affected?

The most common reasons for people falling into debt are losing a job - **20%**, and injury or illness - **15%**.

77% of people the charity dealt with were renters and **24%** of those who rented were in **arrears**.

The average age of people contacting the charity has fallen during the last five years - there are now more people aged between 25-39 and a steady rise in under 25s. This means that **59%** of people contacting the charity are now under 40.

Younger people, particularly those under 25, are more likely to be **renters** and have **insecure jobs**, making them more likely to fall into debt.

As you need to be earning a certain amount to access some types of credit, the debts of younger people tend to be smaller partly due to their lower salaries and the fact that they have had less years to access credit.

Who do they owe money to?

Credit cards, bank overdrafts and personal loans are the most common source of debt.

28% of people contacting the charity had turned to friends and family for loans totalling **£200m**.

The average debt to friends and family was **£4,046**.

More people are on zero hours, part-time and temporary contracts - making them less secure ... this makes it difficult to get by and cope with sudden unexpected expenses.

Pocket money

Pocket money is at its highest since 2007

Average pocket money

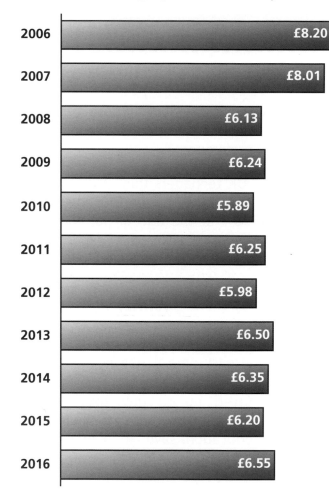

2006	£8.20
2007	£8.01
2008	£6.13
2009	£6.24
2010	£5.89
2011	£6.25
2012	£5.98
2013	£6.50
2014	£6.35
2015	£6.20
2016	£6.55

The Halifax Pocket Money report looks at how much money 8-15 year olds receive and their spending and saving habits. 1,533 British parents of children aged 5-18 were interviewed in January 2016 to find out about their pocket money.

Nine year-olds receive the least on average – £4.68 and 14 year-olds receive the most - £8.03

51% of parents who give pocket money say the main reason is to help their child learn about and manage money independently.

42% of children believe they should receive more pocket money than they do, but 51% believe they receive the right amount of money.

Boys receive 12% more pocket money than girls

Some issues

- Do you think the economy might affect how much pocket money kids get?

- What do you think is the right amount of pocket money to receive?

- Do you think kids should have to 'work' or do tasks to get their spends?

Source: Annual Halifax Pocket Money Survey 2016

lloydsbanking.com

Gender

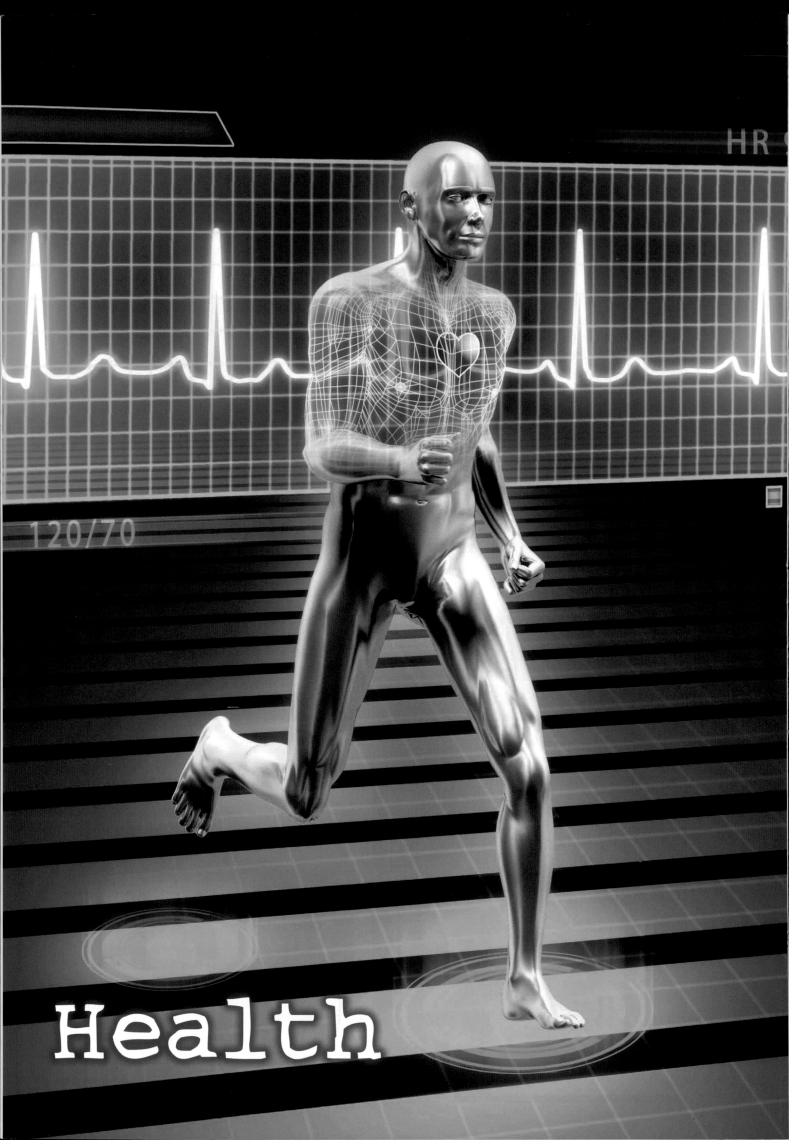

Health

Suicide

Figures suggest that people who feel suicidal can be helped

Myths and facts about suicide

MYTH: YOU HAVE TO BE MENTALLY ILL TO EVEN THINK ABOUT SUICIDE

FACT: Most people have thought of suicide from time to time. However, many people who kill themselves do have mental health problems. Sometimes this is recognised before the person's death.

MYTH MOST SUICIDES HAPPEN IN THE WINTER MONTHS

FACT: Suicide is more common in the spring and summer months.

MYTH: PEOPLE WHO TALK ABOUT SUICIDE AREN'T REALLY SERIOUS AND NOT LIKELY TO ACTUALLY KILL THEMSELVES

FACT: People who kill themselves have often told someone that they do not feel life is worth living or that they have no future. Some may have actually said they want to die – it is very important that everyone who says they feel suicidal be treated seriously.

MYTH: ONCE A PERSON HAS MADE A SERIOUS SUICIDE ATTEMPT, THAT PERSON IS UNLIKELY TO MAKE ANOTHER

FACT: People who have attempted to kill themselves are significantly more likely to eventually die by suicide than the rest of the population.

MYTH: PEOPLE WHO ARE SUICIDAL WANT TO DIE

FACT: The majority do not actually want to die; they just do not want to live the life they have. This important fact means it is vital to talk through other options at the right time.

MYTH: PEOPLE WHO THREATEN SUICIDE ARE JUST ATTENTION SEEKING AND SHOULDN'T BE TAKEN SERIOUSLY

FACT: People may well talk about their feelings because they want support in dealing with them. In this sense it may be that they do indeed want attention in which case giving that attention may save their life.

MYTH: IF A PERSON IS SERIOUS ABOUT KILLING THEMSELVES THEN THERE IS NOTHING YOU CAN DO

FACT: Feeling suicidal is often a temporary state of mind. Whilst someone may feel low or distressed for a sustained period the actual suicidal crisis can be relatively short term.

MYTH: TALKING ABOUT SUICIDE IS A BAD IDEA AS IT MAY GIVE SOMEONE THE IDEA TO TRY IT

FACT: By asking directly about suicide you give that person permission to tell you how they feel – people often say that it was a huge relief to be able to talk about their suicidal thoughts. Once someone starts talking they have a greater chance of discovering alternatives to suicide.

What is suicide?

Suicide is the act of a person willingly ending their own life.

There were **6,122** suicides of people aged 10 and over registered in the UK in 2014. This is a **2% decrease** over 2013.

The high rates of male suicide have led to an increase in suicide prevention strategies and support targeted at men.

The **male** suicide rate **decreased** from **17.8 deaths** in 2013 to **16.8 deaths** per 100,000 in 2014, while the **female** suicide rate **increased** from **4.8** to **5.2 deaths** per 100,000.

All suicides are certified by a coroner following an inquest. Because registration of the death can take months or even years, the figures in the charts below are the number of suicides registered in a year, not the actual number of suicides in that year.

> **Overall suicide rates per 100,000 population, by UK country**

Looking at numbers of suicides in each UK country can be misleading due to different population sizes, so rates per 100,000 are used to give a truer picture of where suicide is more prevalent. The **UK** rate was **10.8 deaths** per 100,000 population in 2014.

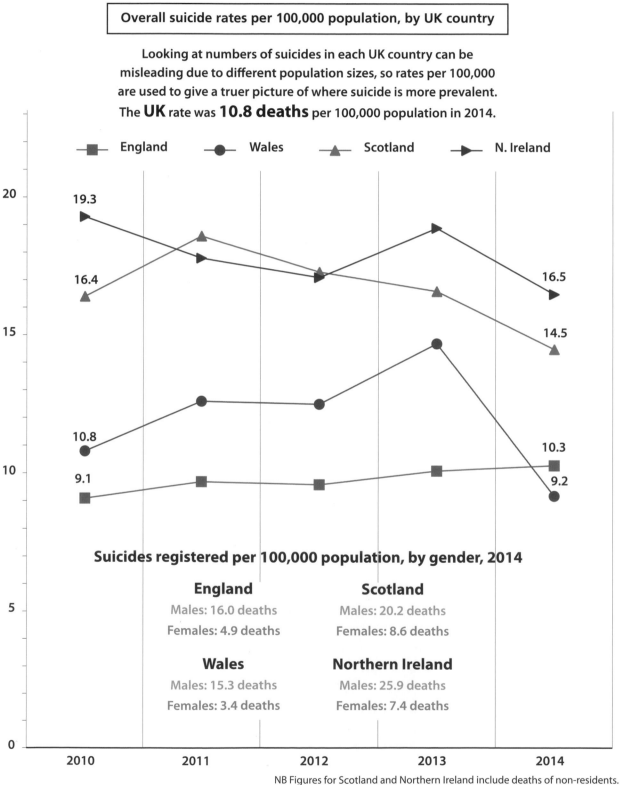

Legend: ■ England ● Wales ▲ Scotland ➤ N. Ireland

Data labels: 19.3, 16.4, 10.8, 9.1, 16.5, 14.5, 10.3, 9.2

Suicides registered per 100,000 population, by gender, 2014

England
Males: 16.0 deaths
Females: 4.9 deaths

Scotland
Males: 20.2 deaths
Females: 8.6 deaths

Wales
Males: 15.3 deaths
Females: 3.4 deaths

Northern Ireland
Males: 25.9 deaths
Females: 7.4 deaths

X-axis: 2010, 2011, 2012, 2013, 2014

NB Figures for Scotland and Northern Ireland include deaths of non-residents. Figures for England and Wales exclude deaths of non-residents.

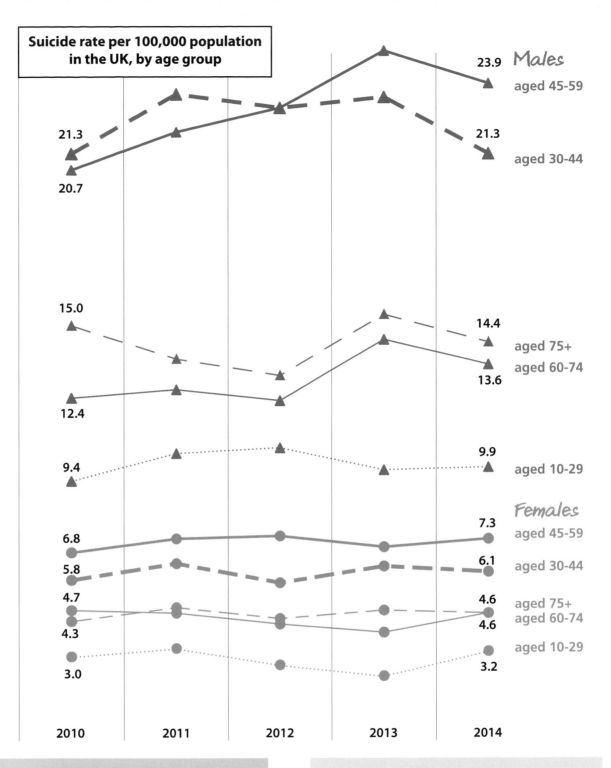

Suicide rate per 100,000 population in the UK, by age group

Males

	2010				2014	
aged 45-59	20.7				23.9	
aged 30-44	21.3				21.3	
aged 75+	15.0				14.4	
aged 60-74	12.4				13.6	
aged 10-29	9.4				9.9	

Females

	2010				2014	
aged 45-59	6.8				7.3	
aged 30-44	5.8				6.1	
aged 75+	4.7				4.6	
aged 60-74	4.3				4.6	
aged 10-29	3.0				3.2	

2010   2011   2012   2013   2014

Helpful organisations

PAPYRUS
www.papyrus-uk.org

Samaritans
www.samaritans.org

Survivors of Bereavement by Suicide
www.uk-sobs.org.uk

CALM
www.thecalmzone.net

Mind
www.mind.org.uk

Some issues

- Which myths about suicide are the least helpful in dealing with the problem?

- It appears that suicide prevention strategies for men are having some effect. How much do you know about these strategies?

- Can you think of any reasons for the big difference in male and female rates of suicide?

Source: Samaritans www.samaritans.org
Office for National Statistics © Crown copyright 2016 www.ons.gov.uk

Mental disorders

Mental disorders are on the rise and young women are a high risk group

Common mental health disorders (CMD) include depression, anxiety disorders, panic disorder, obsessive-compulsive disorder, post-traumatic stress disorder and phobias.

Since 2000, overall rates of CMD in England steadily increased in women and remained largely stable in men.

Young women have emerged as a high-risk group, with high rates of CMD, self-harm, and positive screens for post-traumatic stress disorder (PTSD) and bipolar disorder.

The gap between young women and young men increased.

Disorders were more common in people living alone, in poor physical health, and not employed. People unable to work due to poor health or disability, experienced particularly high rates of all the disorders.

Those reporting a Common Mental Disorder within the past week, by year and gender, %

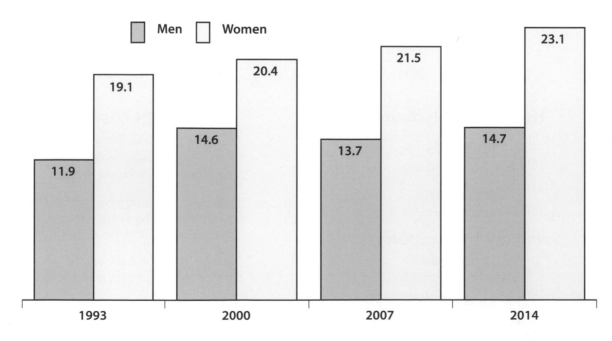

Men Women

	1993	2000	2007	2014
Men	11.9	14.6	13.7	14.7
Women	19.1	20.4	21.5	23.1

The survey of both treated and untreated psychiatric disorders in the English adult population (aged 16 and over), takes place every seven years. 7,500 people aged 16 or more were interviewed, including people who do not use mental health services.

The Clinical Interview Schedule – (CIS-R) is a way of measuring common mental disorders. A score of 18+ indicates severe symptoms that almost certainly need treatment.

Those who scored 18 or more for the CIS-R Score in the past week, by age and gender, %

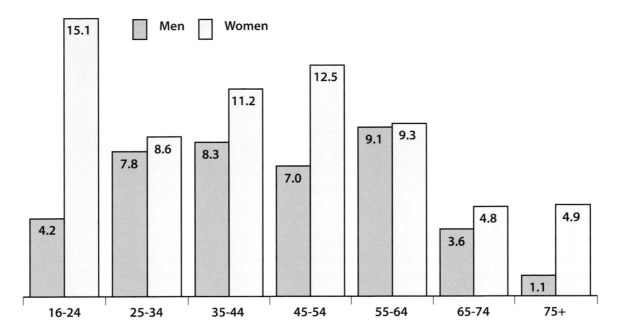

Men   Women

Age	16-24	25-34	35-44	45-54	55-64	65-74	75+
Men	4.2	7.8	8.3	7.0	9.1	3.6	1.1
Women	15.1	8.6	11.2	12.5	9.3	4.8	4.9

The overall increase in CMD was caused by an increase in women suffering from these symptoms. Women were also more likely to experience severe symptoms. These occurred in **10%** of **women** but only **6%** of **men**.

19.7% of 16 to 24 year old women reported having self-harmed at some point in their lives, compared to **6.4%** of the general population. Most did not seek professional help afterwards. People who start to self-harm when they are young risk continuing to use it as a way to cope; there is a risk that the behaviour will spread to other people; and also that this behaviour may lead on to a higher risk of suicide.

Between 2000 and 2014, reports of self-harm among 16- to 24-year-olds doubled in **men** to **7.9%** and trebled in **women** to **19.7%**

The rises could be due to people feeling more able to disclose that they had self-harmed, but it is also possible that increased reporting of self-harm reflects a real increase in the behaviour according to the report.

Incidents of self-harm among 16-24 year olds, by gender and year, %

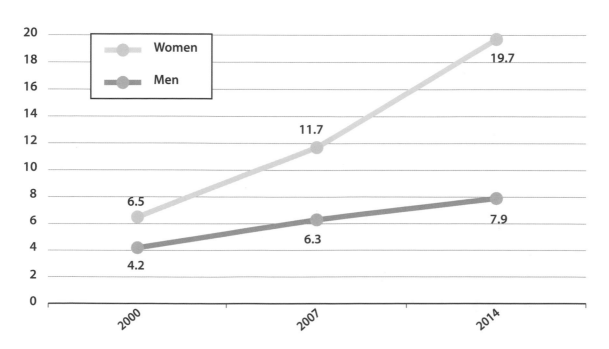

A diagnosis for Post-Traumatic Stress Disorder (PTSD) means that someone has been actually involved in, witnessed or been confronted with a danger to life, or with death, serious injury or threat (to them or others) which is accompanied by feelings of intense fear, horror, or helplessness.

Screening positive for post-traumatic stress disorder, by gender and age, %

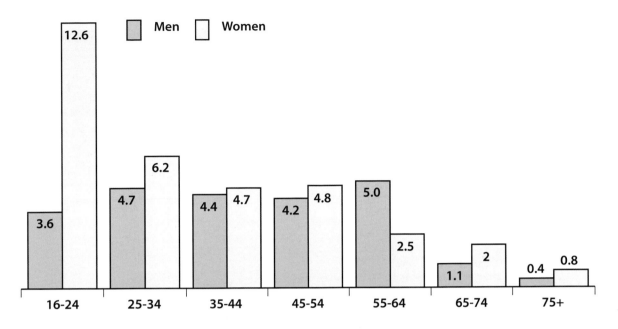

The Social Media Age

"These figures highlight worrying trends, particularly regarding the growing number of young women accessing mental health treatment. Society is changing – even in the last seven years, social media, for example, has increased in popularity and the number of platforms people might be present on has multiplied.

"As a result, young people are facing unprecedented pressures, not just over the emergence of cyberbullying and revenge porn, but constant exposure to unattainable aspirations of what they should look like, and be like."

Prof Maureen Baker, chair of the Royal College of GPs

Where to find help:

In the UK and Ireland the Samaritans can be contacted on 116 123.

You can call Mind, the mental health charity on 0800 123 3393 or text 86463

If you are suffering with panic call No Panic, 0844 967 4848 (daily, 10am-10pm)

You can find useful resources at:

mentalhealth.org.uk
youngminds.org.uk

Some issues

- Why do you think more young women suffer than young men?

- What can young people do to help other young people to cope?

- Do agree that social media contributes towards the increase in mental disorders?

- How do some young people enjoy social media and avoid potential problems?

Source: Mental Health and Wellbeing in England, NHS Digital
www.nhs.uk

Eating disorders

Anyone can suffer with an eating disorder but help is out there

The facts:

Eating disorders can affect someone not only **physically** but can also affect their **mental state** and their **ability to interact with others**.

A person with an eating disorder may focus excessively on their weight, body shape and image. They may appear to have an **abnormal attitude towards food**, which will affect their behaviour and eating habits and can damage their health.

The most common eating disorders are:

Anorexia nervosa - when someone tries to keep their weight as low as possible, for example by starving themselves or exercising excessively.

Bulimia - when someone tries to control their weight by binge eating and then deliberately being sick or using laxatives

Binge eating disorder (BED) - when a person feels compelled to overeat large amounts of food in a short space of time.

Some people overeat for **emotional reasons** such as feeling low, anxious, lonely, or having difficulty dealing with problems. In a survey conducted by b-eat, the eating disorder charity, **87.6%** said they ate for these reasons.

The same survey asked people "Have you sought **advice from your GP** about being overweight?" **48.3%** of people had. But **73.2% of them** said the doctor did not address their emotional health.

Emotional overeating:

- An inability to distinguish physical hunger from emotions.
- Hunger comes on suddenly rather than gradually
- It feels like inescapable craving rather than a hunger pang in the stomach
- It feels like it has to be satisfied immediately

"People need to appreciate this is a devastating condition which affects every aspect of a person's life - I am not a stupid person - I know what I should be doing but am totally overwhelmed by my incapacity to process any excess of emotion other than by using food"

The survey was entitled 'Support for Overeating: your experiences' and was aimed at over 18s who binge eat, compulsively overeat, feel they have emotional eating issues and are overweight, obese or struggling with their weight. It received 1017 responses, including the quote above.

Gender:

Eating disorders are more common in females than in males. Research shows that only **9.2%** of those admitted to hospital with eating disorders were male.

Other research, however, indicates that up to **25%** of sufferers are males. The difference in figures may come about because people **presume** that men do not suffer from eating disorders and therefore they are misdiagnosed. Another reason might be that men do not come forward to seek help.

Treatment:

After a diagnosis, there are many therapies that can help people recover. These include therapies such as cognitive behaviour therapy (CBT) family therapy and self-help programmes.

The most severe cases can involve extended periods of treatment within hospital.

The aim of treatment is not always for a full recovery and for all symptoms to disappear. Instead the aim is to focus on improvements in coping in everyday life. This allows patients to have a positive focus on improving their quality of life rather than focusing solely on their weight.

Hospital admissions for an eating disorder,
by gender, ages from 10 - 24 years old February 2015 - January 2016

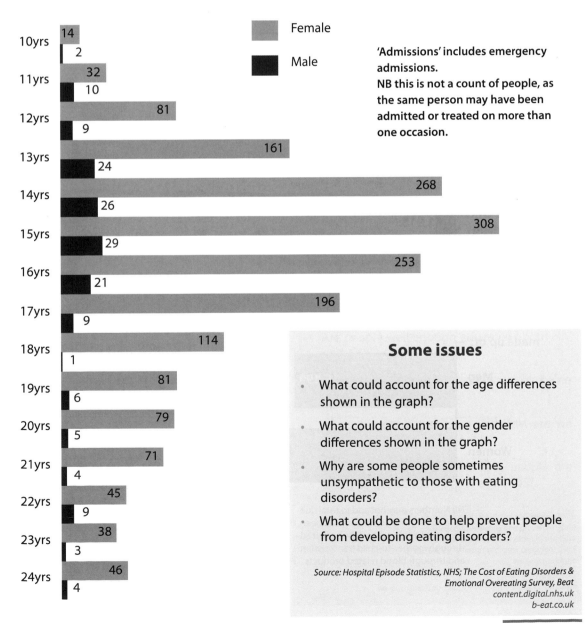

Female

Male

'Admissions' includes emergency admissions.
NB this is not a count of people, as the same person may have been admitted or treated on more than one occasion.

Age	Female	Male
10yrs	14	2
11yrs	32	10
12yrs	81	9
13yrs	161	24
14yrs	268	26
15yrs	308	29
16yrs	253	21
17yrs	196	9
18yrs	114	1
19yrs	81	6
20yrs	79	5
21yrs	71	4
22yrs	45	9
23yrs	38	3
24yrs	46	4

Some issues

- What could account for the age differences shown in the graph?

- What could account for the gender differences shown in the graph?

- Why are some people sometimes unsympathetic to those with eating disorders?

- What could be done to help prevent people from developing eating disorders?

Source: Hospital Episode Statistics, NHS; The Cost of Eating Disorders & Emotional Overeating Survey, Beat
content.digital.nhs.uk
b-eat.co.uk

Number of **previous** legal abortions for women **resident** in England & Wales, by age group, 2015

Number of previous abortions	Age group						Total
	Under 16	16 & 17	18 & 19	20 - 24	25 - 29	30 or over	
None	1,812	7,321	13,670	34,474	24,707	33,546	115,530
1	41	604	2,361	13,364	14,329	19,991	50,690
2	0	40	275	2,923	4,598	6,569	14,405
3	0	3	30	578	1,180	1,853	3,644
4	0	0	2	142	332	554	1,030
5	0	0	1	32	95	194	322
6	0	0	2	8	32	66	108
7	0	0	0	1	15	29	45
8 or more	0	0	0	3	12	35	50
Total	1,853	7.968	16,341	51,525	45,300	62,837	185,824

In 2015, **38%** of women in **England and Wales** and **31%** of women in **Scotland** undergoing abortions had previously had one or more previous abortions.

NB Percentages are subject to rounding and totals may not agree with the sum of the component figures shown

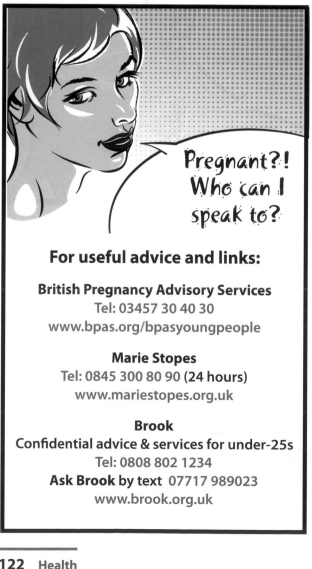

Pregnant?! Who can I speak to?

For useful advice and links:

British Pregnancy Advisory Services
Tel: 03457 30 40 30
www.bpas.org/bpasyoungpeople

Marie Stopes
Tel: 0845 300 80 90 (24 hours)
www.mariestopes.org.uk

Brook
Confidential advice & services for under-25s
Tel: 0808 802 1234
Ask Brook by text 07717 989023
www.brook.org.uk

"I didn't think that I would get pregnant... I was only 15 and really worried.

I went to a clinic where they listened to me and told me what my choices were. I decided to have an abortion and for me I think it was the best decision."

Hannah, age 19

Some issues

- Why do different parts of the UK have different laws regarding abortion?

- Most abortions are carried out in the very early stages of pregnancy. Why is this important?

- What do you think of the current laws on abortion?

Source: Department of Health Abortion Statistics, England & Wales: 2015
© Crown copyright 2016 www.dh.gov.uk
Termination of Pregnancy Statistics - NHS National Services Scotland
www.nhsnss.org
British Pregnancy Advisory Service www.bpas.org/bpasyoungpeople

Internet

Sport & leisure

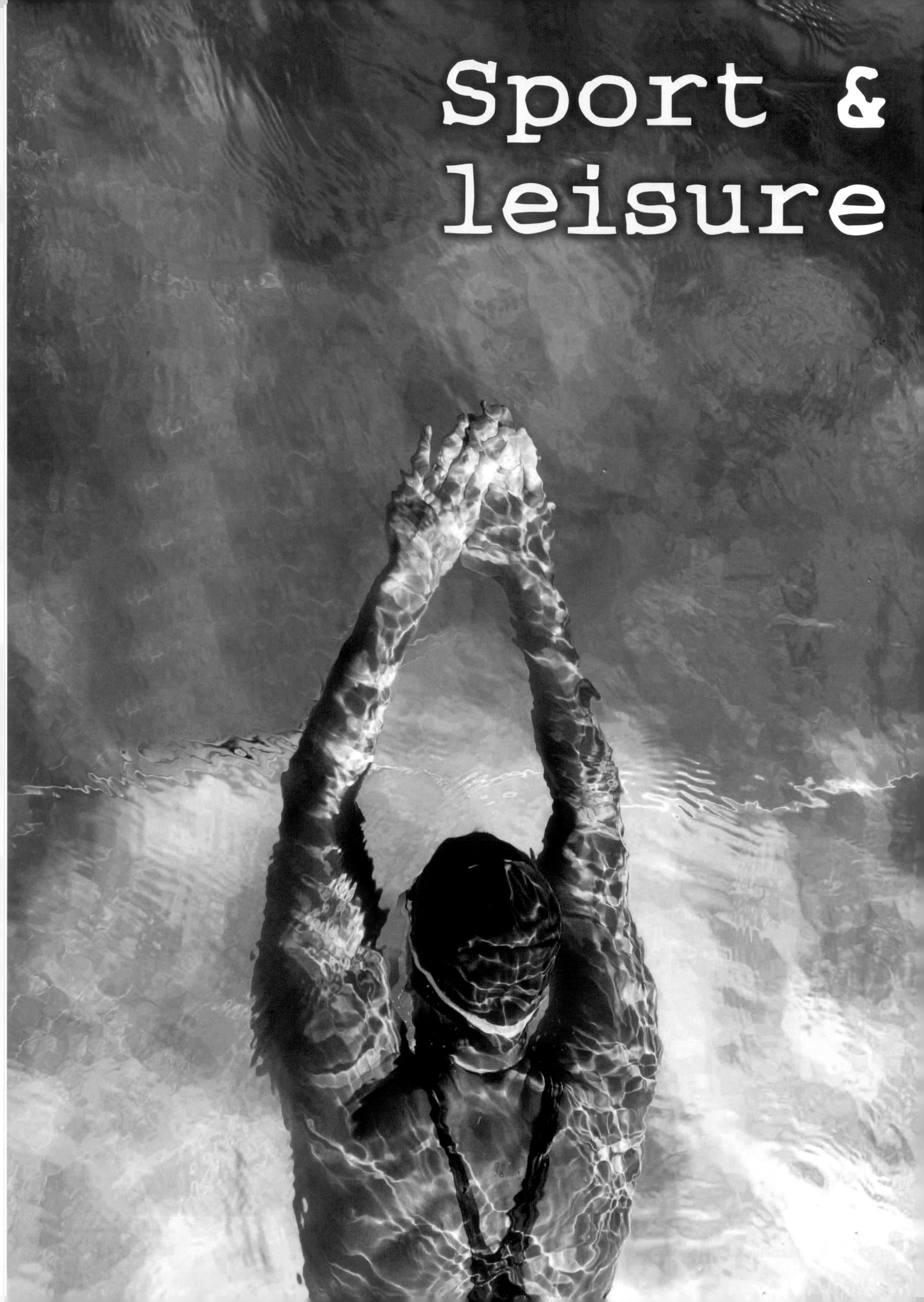

Olympics: who won?

Official Olympic medal rankings tell us who won most gold medals – but there are other ways of looking at the achievements

Top ten Olympic medal winning countries, official ranking by gold medals won, Rio, 2016

	Gold	Silver	Bronze	Total
United States	46	37	38	121
GB/UK	27	23	17	67
China	26	18	26	70
Russia	19	18	19	56
Germany	17	10	15	42
Japan	12	8	21	41
France	10	18	14	42
South Korea	9	3	9	21
Italy	8	12	8	28
Australia	8	11	10	29

The Netherlands and Hungary both also won 8 golds but their medal total was lower than Australia's.

Photo: Tim Hipps

Mohamed "Mo" Farah, CBE is the most successful British track athlete in modern Olympic Games history.

He is the 2012 and 2016 Olympic gold medallist in both the 5,000m and 10,000m.

He is the second athlete in modern Olympic Games history (after Lasse Virén of Finland) to successfully defend the 5,000m and 10,000m titles.

British success

130 British Olympians from a squad of 366 have won a medal - 35.5% of the team

Male medal winners **71** out 202 - 35.1%

Female medal winners **59** out of 164 - 36%

Average age of Britain's medallists **28.1**

17 titles from London 2012 were defended, including six cycling events

The oldest medallist for team GB (Nick Skelton) **58**

Britain won medals in **19** different sports, more than any other country

13 GB Olympians won more than one medal

Britain won **67** medals in Rio - the first host country to increase its medal total at the next Games

British Olympians who won more than one medal:

Cycling: Jason Kenny - 3 gold, Laura Trott - 2 gold, Mark Cavendish - 1 gold, 1 silver, Callum Skinner - 1 gold 1 silver

Athletics: Mo Farah - 2 gold

Swimming: Adam Peaty - 1 gold, 1 silver, Duncan Scott, Jazmin Carlin - 2 silver, James Guy- 2 silver

Gymnastics: Max Whitlock - 2 gold, 1 bronze

Diving: Jack Laugher - 1 gold, 1 silver

Canoeing: Liam Heath - 1 gold, 1 silver

Equestrian: Charlotte Dujardin - 1 gold, 1 silver

Some issues

- Does success at the Olympic Games inspire people to take up sport? Or to achieve more?

- Does Olympic success have any wider effects outside of sport?

- The alternative medals tables show the ways in which the Olympics are not 'fair'. Can sport ever be really fair?

- Are Olympic medals worth the money spent on them?

Source: www.medalspercapita.com
UKSport: www.uksport.gov.uk/everyroadtorio

Paralympics: who won?

The London 2012 and Rio 2016 paralympics were a success - but do such events improve daily life for people with disabilities?

In the first games to be known as Paralympics (Rome 1960), 400 athletes from 21 nations took part in nine events.

In 2016, more than 11,000 athletes competed in 22 sports. This was the year that the sports Para-Canoe and Para-Triathlon made their debuts.

Paralympics 2016, official ranking by gold medals won, top ten countries

Rank by gold	Country	Gold	Silver	Bronze
1	China	107	81	51
2	Great Britain	64	39	44
3	Ukraine	41	37	39
4	United States	40	44	31
5	Australia	22	30	29
6	Germany	18	25	14
7	Netherlands	17	19	26
8	Brazil	14	29	29
9	Italy	10	14	15
10	Poland	9	18	12

Great Britain won a total of
147 medals -
47 of these were in **swimming**,
33 in **athletics**,
21 in **cycling** and
11 in **equestrian**.

For the Tokyo games in 2020, most sports have received extra funding. However swimming has had its budget cut and wheelchair rugby will receive no financial support.

Swimmer **Bethany Firth** was the most decorated British athlete with **3 golds** and **1 silver**.

Cyclist Sarah Storey also set a Paralympic and world record.

Photo: Kafuffle

Do the Paralympics have the power to improve attitudes to disability?

Before the start of the Paralympics in Rio, the charity Scope published findings of a poll which asked disabled people whether the Paralympics can change attitudes to disability and asked what life is like if you're disabled in 2016.

The survey of over 1,000 disabled people found that they were positive about the way the games could change attitudes in the short term by increasing the visibility of disabled people and celebrating Paralympians as sporting equals.

However, long-term positive impacts were less certain. Four years on from the huge success of London 2012 disabled people continue to face negative attitudes.

1 in 5 disabled people think that the accessibility of pubs, restaurants, clubs and shops has improved (23%), or transport (21%)

Just one fifth (19%) of disabled people think Britain is a better place to be disabled than four years ago.

82% of disabled people believe the Paralympics make disabled people more visible in wider society.

Disabled people continue to face huge barriers to work with just 15% saying employer attitudes have improved since London 2012.

78% of disabled people say the Paralympics have a positive impact on attitudes to disability.

Nearly 80% of disabled people say there has been no change in the way people act towards them.

Some issues

- Did the Paralympics in London and in Rio alter your own attitude towards people with a disability?

- How can everyday life be made easier for a range of people with disabilities?

- Should the media make more effort to cover sports that feature disabled people?

Source: blog.scope.org.uk/2016/09/05/do-the-paralympics-have-the-power-to-improve-attitudes-to-disability

www.paralympic.org

The cost of seeing one home goal

(Calculated by dividing the cost of the cheapest season ticket by the number of home goals scored in season 2015/16)

Club	Cost
Arsenal	£32.71
Bournemouth	£23.91
Chelsea	£23.44
Crystal Palace	£22.11
Tottenham	£21.86
Liverpool	£21.52
West Brom	£19.95
Man Utd	£19.70
Watford	£19.25
West Ham	£18.16
Sunderland	£16.09
Southampton	£13.87
Stoke	£13.36
Everton	£12.69
Middlesbrough	£11.68
Hull City	£11.30
Leicester	£10.43
Burnley	£8.66
Man City	£6.36

NB Swansea City did not take part in the 2015/16 survey

For your programme, a pie and a cup of tea **Chelsea** will charge you a total of **£6.50** - **£3** for a programme, **£2.50** for a pie and **£1** for a tea.

West Ham, on the other hand, charges **£3.50** for a programme, **£4.10** for a pie and **£2.40** for a tea - a total of **£10**.

Some issues

- Could you afford to go to matches regularly?

- Is a season ticket good value or do clubs exploit their most loyal supporters?

- Can you think of any reasons why the cost of watching football varies so much?

- "Rich Premier League Clubs are getting richer, other clubs cannot compete". Would you agree or disagree that this is a problem for football?

- Are the tickets for women's football too cheap?

Source: BBC Price of Football 2016
www.bbc.co.uk/sport/football/37953195

Statista: www.statista.com/chart/6796/goals-come-with-a-hefty-price-tag-at-the-emirates

War & conflict

64 countries and territories where incidents of explosive violence were reported in 2015

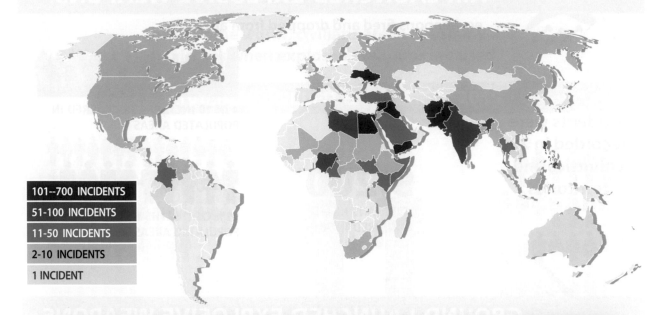

101--700 INCIDENTS
51-100 INCIDENTS
11-50 INCIDENTS
2-10 INCIDENTS
1 INCIDENT

THE MOST DANGEROUS PLACES TO BE A CIVILIAN

Top 10 countries and territories with the highest reported number of civilian casualties from explosive violence

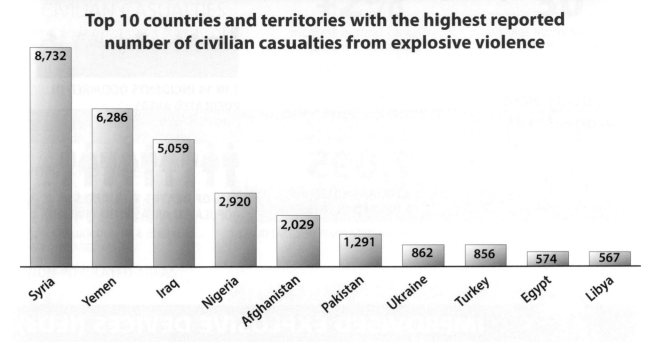

Syria	Yemen	Iraq	Nigeria	Afghanistan	Pakistan	Ukraine	Turkey	Egypt	Libya
8,732	6,286	5,059	2,920	2,029	1,291	862	856	574	567

2016 update

In September 2016 alone, there were **4,172** deaths and injuries from explosive violence in 24 countries.

Of the deaths and injuries, **72%** (3,028) were civilians.

Syria continued to be the worst affected country with **at least 1,951** civilian deaths and injuries from explosive violence.

Some issues

- Why are civilians, rather than military personnel, more likely to be victims?

- What could be done to protect civilians in areas of conflict?

- How can people in peaceful areas understand the problems in war zones?

- What should people in peaceful areas do to help?

Source: © Action on Armed Violence, April 2016 www.aoav.org.uk

Wider world

World optimism

By many measures, the world is getting better

In most places the chance of not getting killed by another human, life expectancy, poverty, democracy and the rule of law have all improved significantly over the past 200 years.

YouGov research of 18,235 people found that out of 17 countries, China was by far the most likely to be optimistic about the future of the planet. The percentage of optimists in China is four times the 10% global average.

% who think generally that, all things considered, the world is getting better

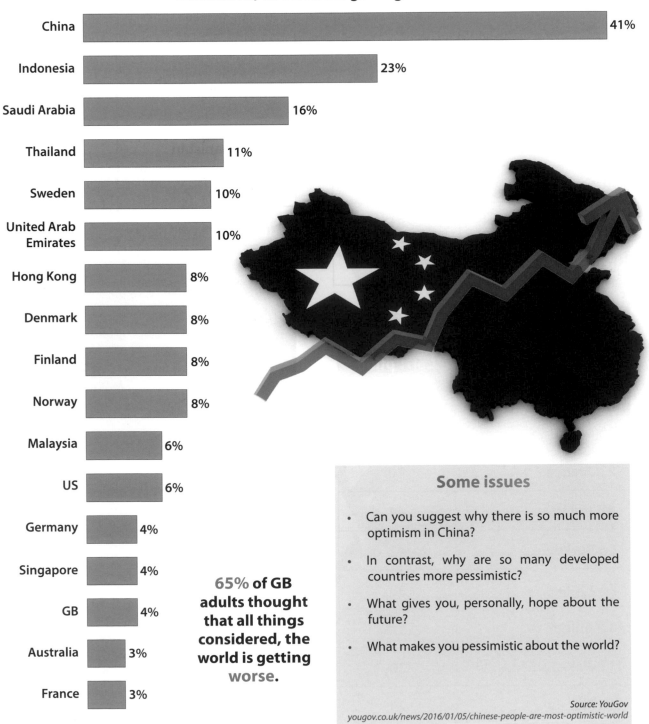

Country	%
China	41%
Indonesia	23%
Saudi Arabia	16%
Thailand	11%
Sweden	10%
United Arab Emirates	10%
Hong Kong	8%
Denmark	8%
Finland	8%
Norway	8%
Malaysia	6%
US	6%
Germany	4%
Singapore	4%
GB	4%
Australia	3%
France	3%

65% of GB adults thought that all things considered, the world is getting worse.

Some issues

- Can you suggest why there is so much more optimism in China?

- In contrast, why are so many developed countries more pessimistic?

- What gives you, personally, hope about the future?

- What makes you pessimistic about the world?

Source: YouGov
yougov.co.uk/news/2016/01/05/chinese-people-are-most-optimistic-world

Work

Hours and earnings

There is a huge gap between the average earnings of the highest and lowest paid people

Hours worked

In 2015 full-time employees worked an average of **39.1** paid hours per week (including overtime).

Earnings

The average **UK** earnings were **£527.70** per week for full-time employees.

Regional differences

The highest earnings per week at **£659.90**, were in **London**. This was **£132 more** than the UK average. (Many employees in London work in high-paying occupations or have a London Allowance to account for the extra cost of living in the capital).

The lowest earnings were in **Wales**, at **£473.40**.

Proportion of people in the labour market, October to December 2015

(**Economically inactive** people are not in employment but not classed as unemployed because they are not seeking work. They might, for example, be studying, looking after family or long-term sick)

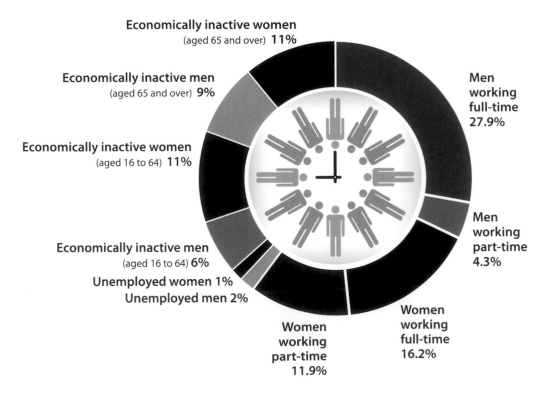

Economically inactive women (aged 65 and over) **11%**

Economically inactive men (aged 65 and over) **9%**

Economically inactive women (aged 16 to 64) **11%**

Economically inactive men (aged 16 to 64) **6%**

Unemployed women **1%**
Unemployed men **2%**

Women working part-time **11.9%**

Women working full-time **16.2%**

Men working part-time **4.3%**

Men working full-time **27.9%**

Differences in earnings

The average hourly pay for full-time employees in the UK was £12. People in the lowest 10% of earners were paid £7 an hour on average while those in the highest 10% received £26 per hour.

The wide difference in earnings is made clear when we look at what percentage of the median (the middle point of the range) each group earned. The lowest earners received 57% of the mid-point wage while the highest earners received 214%.

There were some differences between the distribution of earnings by age for men and women

Men's weekly earnings were highest in the 40 to 49 age group while women's earnings were highest in the 30 to 39 age group.

Median full-time gross weekly earnings by gender and age group in the UK

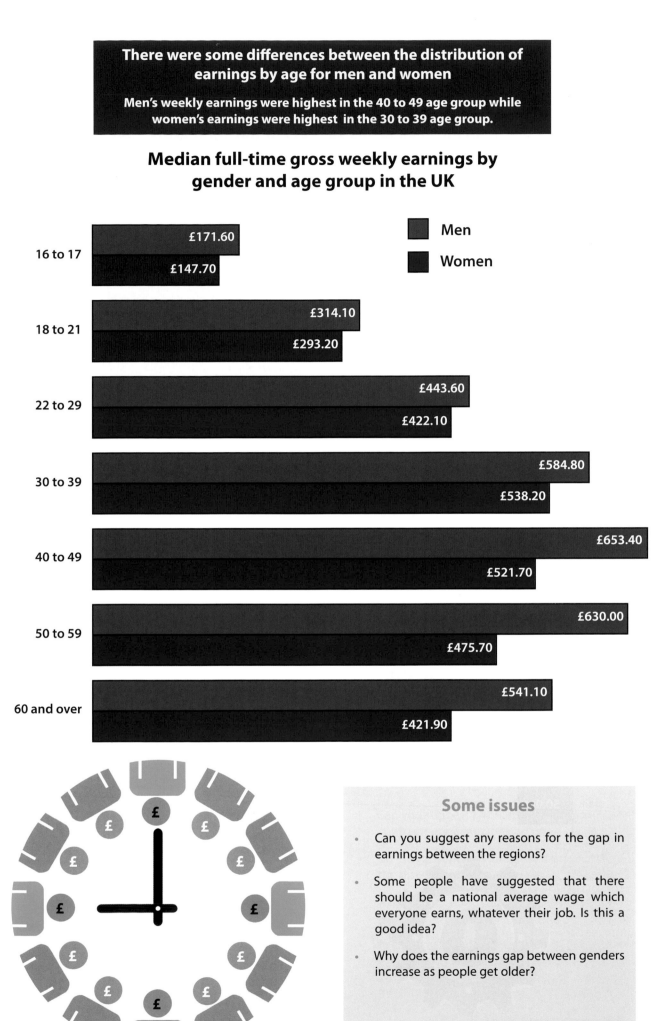

■ Men
■ Women

16 to 17
£171.60
£147.70

18 to 21
£314.10
£293.20

22 to 29
£443.60
£422.10

30 to 39
£584.80
£538.20

40 to 49
£653.40
£521.70

50 to 59
£630.00
£475.70

60 and over
£541.10
£421.90

Some issues

- Can you suggest any reasons for the gap in earnings between the regions?

- Some people have suggested that there should be a national average wage which everyone earns, whatever their job. Is this a good idea?

- Why does the earnings gap between genders increase as people get older?

Source: The Annual Survey of Hours and Earnings (ASHE)
© Crown copyright 2015 www.ons.gov.uk

Work and gender

Does your gender affect the work you want to do?

Young people, aged 13-25, were asked whether men or women were more suited to certain activities. They gave a score on a scale of 1-9. Anything between 1-4 was more towards men, 5 was both equally and 6-9 was more towards women.

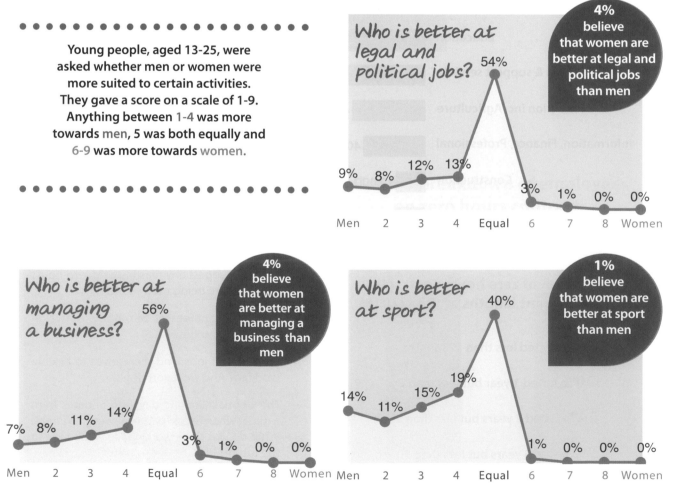

Who is better at legal and political jobs?

4% believe that women are better at legal and political jobs than men

Men	2	3	4	Equal	6	7	8	Women
9%	8%	12%	13%	54%	3%	1%	0%	0%

Who is better at managing a business?

4% believe that women are better at managing a business than men

Men	2	3	4	Equal	6	7	8	Women
7%	8%	11%	14%	56%	3%	1%	0%	0%

Who is better at sport?

1% believe that women are better at sport than men

Men	2	3	4	Equal	6	7	8	Women
14%	11%	15%	19%	40%	1%	0%	0%	0%

What kind of impact do you think your gender will have on your future career prospects?

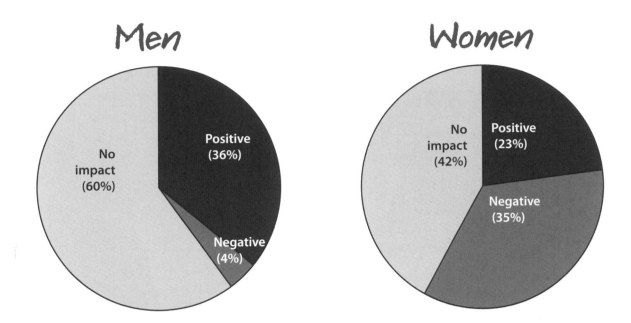

Men

- Positive (36%)
- No impact (60%)
- Negative (4%)

Women

- Positive (23%)
- No impact (42%)
- Negative (35%)

Old stereotypes are changing

Young men and women might possibly believe their gender is affecting their career or work choices since it seems that a lot of people still cling to old-fashioned stereotypes.

However people's ideas do seem to be changing.

For example:
When asked
"Are men better at problem solving?"
82% of respondents said **NO**.

When asked
"Are women better at bringing up children?'
66% of respondents said **NO**.

When asked
"Are men and women equally responsible for household income?"
87% said **YES**.

When asked
"Can gender determine how good somebody is at a job"
81% said **NO**.

When I first started as a film director none of the crew had ever worked for a woman. Some of them were unhappy about it; deliberately putting the camera in the wrong place, pretending not to hear instructions.

Over time it got better, as more women came into the industry into 'male jobs' both on and off the set, social attitudes changed.

Beeban Kidron, British filmmaker. and joint founder of the education charity Filmclub, which helps schools with after-school clubs in the United Kingdom.

Some issues

- How does society influence what jobs men and women think they can and can't do?

- What work would you like to do and do you think your gender will affect your success?

- How could you change people's views about certain jobs and skills being associated with one gender?

Base: 1,101 young people aged 13-25 in the UK

Source: The Gender Report, Ditch The Label
Ditchthelabel.org

Race at work

BAME (Black, Asian and Minority Ethnic) people face prejudice in the race to the top

In the UK today, Black, Asian and Minority Ethnic (BAME) people are under-represented at every management level in the workplace. One in eight of the working-age population is from a BAME background, yet only one in 16 top management positions are held by an ethnic minority person.

Respondents who stated they had experienced or witnessed racial harassment or bullying from managers in the last 5 years, by ethnic group

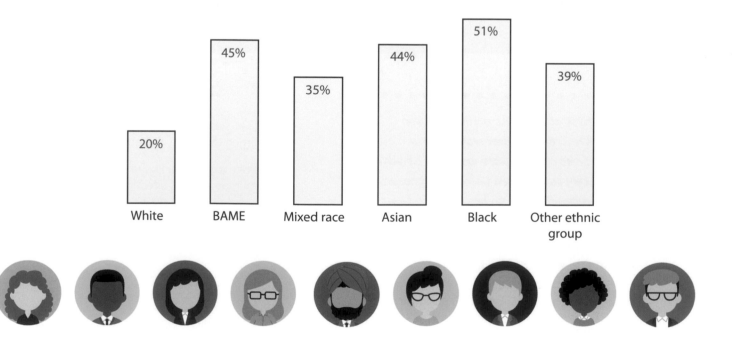

White	BAME	Mixed race	Asian	Black	Other ethnic group
20%	45%	35%	44%	51%	39%

Do people enjoy where they work? All workers were asked if they agreed, neither/nor, or disagreed with the following statements:

I can be myself at work

55% agree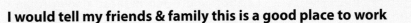

I enjoy working for my organisation

60% agree

I would tell my friends & family this is a good place to work

65% agree

While people overall may appear to be happy,
33% say their career has failed to meet their expectations.
This is higher among Black African (**45%**) and Black Caribbean (**40%**) employees

Dissatisfaction with career development

Percentage answering 'dissatisfied' when asked about their career development to date.

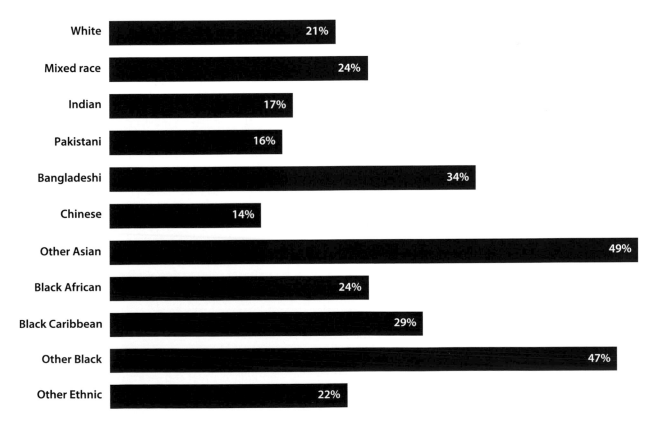

White	21%
Mixed race	24%
Indian	17%
Pakistani	16%
Bangladeshi	34%
Chinese	14%
Other Asian	49%
Black African	24%
Black Caribbean	29%
Other Black	47%
Other Ethnic	22%

There is a clear distinction between ethnic groups on the level of satisfaction they feel about their "career development."

Are all people treated equally?

36%

Across all ethnic groups, **36%** disagree that managers treat all people equally with regards to career progression

Experiences with their manager at work seem to vary by ethnic group.
The percentages who do not believe that managers in their organisation treat all people equally in regard to career progression are:
Black Caribbean **41%**, white **39%** and mixed race **37%** .

Opportunities at work

26% of employees feel they have been overlooked for a promotion in their current organisation. Employees from BAME groups are significantly more likely to feel they have been overlooked for a promotion **(30%)** compared to white employees **(23%)**, and is felt highest among Asian groups **(31%** overall, specifically Pakistani **35%**, and Indian **33%**).

> "Not active discrimination, but just a propensity to look at young white people as having potential, rather than others."
>
> *Female, 54, Mixed (White and Black Caribbean)*

> "I am not in the 'personal group of friends' that get all the promotions and pay rises."
>
> *Female, 51, Chinese*

Some issues

- Are BAME people getting a raw deal in the workplace?

- What obstacles do you think BAME people face in work?

- Whose responsibility is it to make the workplace equal and inclusive for all?

- How can equality at work be improved?

Source: Race at Work, 2015,
The Prince's Responsible Business Network, YouGov
race.bitc.org.uk

Generation work

Young people expect to work longer but are optimistic about their careers

By 2020 Millennials
(who reached adulthood around the year 2000)
will make up over a third of the global workforce

> The Manpower Group carried out research in 25 countries and surveyed 19,000 Millennials.

Make up of the global workforce 2020

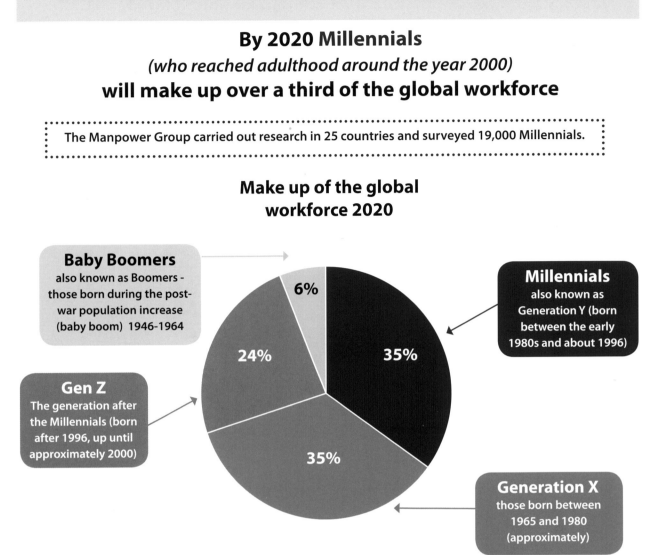

Baby Boomers
also known as Boomers - those born during the post-war population increase (baby boom) 1946-1964

Gen Z
The generation after the Millennials (born after 1996, up until approximately 2000)

6%

24%

35%

35%

Millennials
also known as Generation Y (born between the early 1980s and about 1996)

Generation X
those born between 1965 and 1980 (approximately)

Other nicknames for Millennials

Germany - Generation Maybe - because they seem to have so many possibilities that they cannot commit to anything.

Japan - both "the people who are always doing two things at once" and the relaxed generation (not a compliment in that society).

Spain - Generación Ni Ni - neither, nor - because the economic situation means they can neither work nor study.

UK - Generation Rent, because they cannot get on the housing ladder.

US - Generation Debt, because of the crippling costs of their education.

How many hours do millennials work?

73% of Millennials said they worked **more than 40 hours a week**, and **nearly a quarter** work **over 50 hours**. Millennials in **India** claim the longest working week and **Australians** the shortest. **26%** globally are working in **two or more** paid jobs.

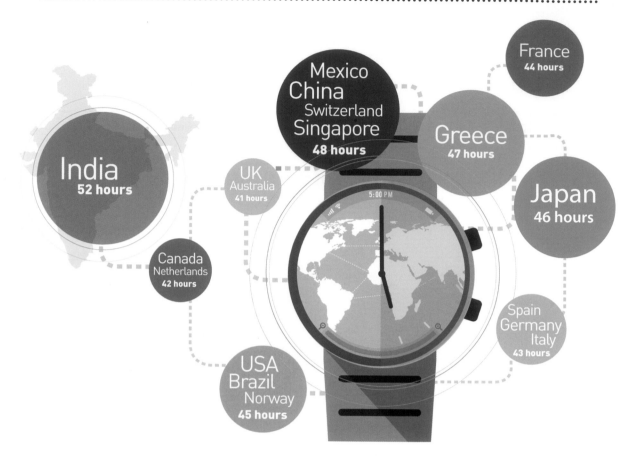

France
44 hours

Mexico
China
Switzerland
Singapore
48 hours

Greece
47 hours

India
52 hours

UK
Australia
41 hours

Japan
46 hours

Canada
Netherlands
42 hours

Spain
Germany
Italy
43 hours

USA
Brazil
Norway
45 hours

Type of work millennials do now and future possibilities

■ How do you work now?   ▨ How would you consider working in the future?

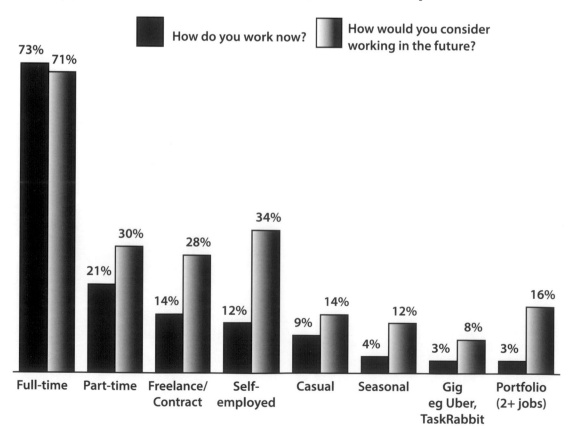

	How do you work now?	How would you consider working in the future?
Full-time	73%	71%
Part-time	21%	30%
Freelance/Contract	14%	28%
Self-employed	12%	34%
Casual	9%	14%
Seasonal	4%	12%
Gig eg Uber, TaskRabbit	3%	8%
Portfolio (2+ jobs)	3%	16%

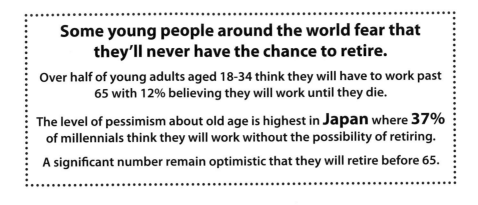

Some young people around the world fear that they'll never have the chance to retire.

Over half of young adults aged 18-34 think they will have to work past 65 with 12% believing they will work until they die.

The level of pessimism about old age is highest in **Japan** where **37%** of millennials think they will work without the possibility of retiring.

A significant number remain optimistic that they will retire before 65.

% of young people aged 18-34 expecting to work until they die

Country	%
Japan	37%
China	18%
Greece	15%
Canada	14%
India	14%
Singapore	14%
Italy	12%
UK	12%
US	12%
Australia	11%
Brazil	10%
Germany	9%
France	8%
Mexico	8%
Spain	3%

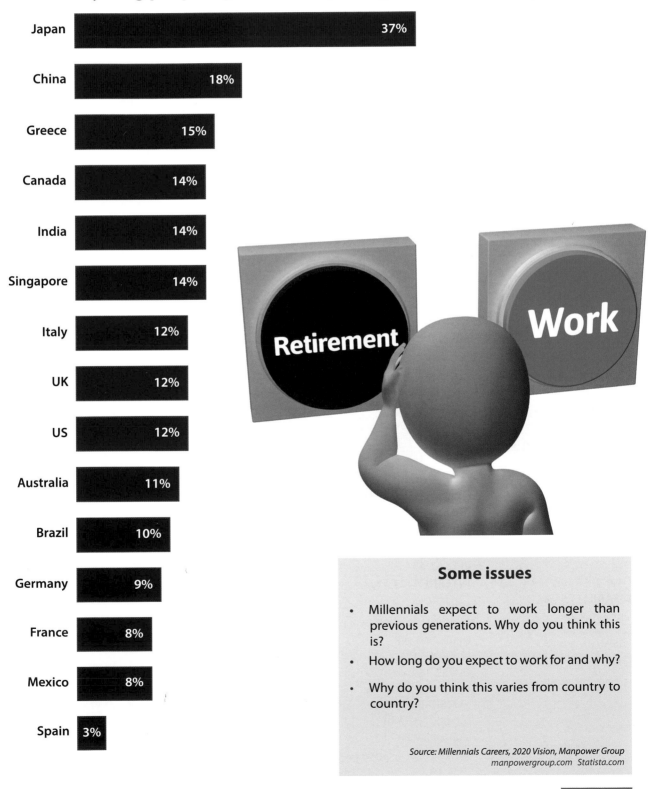

Some issues

- Millennials expect to work longer than previous generations. Why do you think this is?
- How long do you expect to work for and why?
- Why do you think this varies from country to country?

Source: Millennials Careers, 2020 Vision, Manpower Group
manpowergroup.com Statista.com

Index

Entries in **colour** refer to main sections. Page numbers refer to the first page. Most charts contain UK or GB information.

Complete Issues

understanding our world